CHINA'S ENVIRONMENTAL CHALLENGES

D1110858

CHINA'S ENVIRONMENTAL CHALLENGES

Judith Shapiro

polity

Copyright © Judith Shapiro 2012

The right of Judith Shapiro to be identified as Author of this Work has been asserted in accordance with the UK Copyright, Designs and Patents Act 1988.

First published in 2012 by Polity Press

Polity Press
65 Bridge Street
Cambridge CB2 1UR, UK

Polity Press
350 Main Street
Malden, MA 02148, USA

All rights reserved. Except for the quotation of short passages for the purpose of criticism and review, no part of this publication may be reproduced, stored in a retrieval system, or transmitted, in any form or by any means, electronic, mechanical, photocopying, recording or otherwise, without the prior permission of the publisher.

ISBN-13: 978-0-7456-6090-5
ISBN-13: 978-0-7456-6091-2(pb)

A catalogue record for this book is available from the British Library.

Typeset in 11.5 on 15 pt Adobe Jenson Pro
by Toppan Best-set Premedia Limited
Printed and bound in the USA by Edwards Brothers, Inc.

The publisher has used its best endeavours to ensure that the URLs for external websites referred to in this book are correct and active at the time of going to press. However, the publisher has no responsibility for the websites and can make no guarantee that a site will remain live or that the content is or will remain appropriate.

Every effort has been made to trace all copyright holders, but if any have been inadvertently overlooked the publisher will be pleased to include any necessary credits in any subsequent reprint or edition.

For further information on Polity, visit our website: www.politybooks.com

Contents

Chronology

March 1959	Tibetan uprising in Lhasa; Dalai Lama flees to India
1959–1961	Three Hard Years, widespread famine with tens of millions of deaths
Early 1960s	Sino-Soviet split
1962	Sino-Indian War
October 1964	First PRC atomic bomb detonation
1966–1976	Great Proletarian Cultural Revolution; Mao reasserts power
February 1972	President Richard Nixon visits China; 'Shanghai Communiqué' pledges to normalize U.S.–China relations
June 1972	United Nations Conference on the Human Environment held in Stockholm
July 1976	Tangshan earthquake kills hundreds of thousands
September 1976	Death of Mao Zedong
October 1976	Ultra-Leftist Gang of Four arrested and sentenced
December 1978	Deng Xiaoping assumes power; launches Four Modernizations and economic reforms
1978	One-child family planning policy introduced
1979	U.S. and China establish formal diplomatic ties
1979	PRC invades Vietnam
January 1981	PRC ratifies 1973 Convention on International Trade in Endangered Species (CITES)
1982	Census reports PRC population at more than one billion
December 1984	Sino-British Joint Declaration agrees to return Hong Kong to China in 1997
1989	Tiananmen Square protests culminate in June 4 military crack-down

June 1991	PRC ratifies 1987 Montreal Protocol on Substances that Deplete the Ozone Layer
December 1991	PRC ratifies 1989 Basel Convention on the Control of Transboundary Movements of Hazardous Wastes and Their Disposal
April 1992	National People's Congress formally approves Three Gorges Dam
June 1992	United Nations Conference on Environment and Development held in Rio
1992	Deng Xiaoping's Southern Inspection Tour re-energizes economic reforms
1993–2002	Jiang Zemin is president of PRC, continues economic growth agenda
1998	Yangzi River floods kill thousands, leave millions homeless, prompt logging ban
March 1998	State Environmental Protection Administration (SEPA) created
November 2001	WTO accepts China as member
August 2002	World Summit on Sustainable Development held in Johannesburg; PRC ratifies 1997 Kyoto Protocol to the United Nations Framework Convention on Climate Change
2003–2013	Hu Jintao is president of PRC
2002–2003	SARS outbreak
2006	PRC supplants U.S. as largest gross CO_2 emitter; Three Gorges Dam mostly complete
March 2008	State Environmental Protection Administration upgraded to Ministry of Environmental Protection
May 2008	Sichuan earthquake kills tens of thousands
August 2008	Summer Olympic Games in Beijing

Preface

I first visited the People's Republic of China in the summer of 1977. United States–China relations had not yet been normalized, Mao Zedong had been dead less than a year, and political posters plastered everywhere showed the Chairman lying on his sickbed with his chosen successor Hua Guofeng at his side, saying "With You in Charge, I am at Ease." Hua would only hold power until December 1978. A reformist government followed under the leadership of Deng Xiaoping, who returned from political exile and persecution to revolutionize China as profoundly as Mao did in 1949 when the Chinese Communist Party's army defeated Chiang Kai-shek's Nationalist Kuomintang (KMT) and drove it and its followers to Taiwan. Little did I know then, at the age of 24, that the parades and celebrations I witnessed in Shanghai marked the beginning of Deng's political rehabilitation. Nor did I understand that this political "opening" was about to transform China, the world, and also my own life, providing me with the opportunity to be among the first 40 Americans to teach English there, along with a few resident foreign Maoists who had managed to survive the turmoil of the Cultural Revolution.

China had been profoundly shut away from most of the outside world since the Sino-Soviet split in the early 1960s. What the West knew about the Mao years was limited largely to interviews with refugees conducted by scholars and government officials in Hong Kong, and glowing reports from leftwing "friends of China." When I was at university and graduate school in the 1970s, the United States was reeling from the unpopular Vietnam War. Many American young people were highly critical of the U.S. government and skeptical of its claims that our traditional enemies, China among them, could possibly be as bad as claimed. We knew vaguely about "people's communes," which sounded fascinating at a time when our domestic counter-culture movement was also experimenting with collective living. We also knew that in China it was said that "Women Hold up Half the Sky," a compelling slogan for Western feminists who were expanding their intellectual, political, and personal influence and becoming a truly popular women's movement. Through "ping-pong diplomacy," or friendly sports matches intended to break down political barriers, and the limited cultural exchanges that followed the famous 1972 Nixon and Kissinger visit, we caught televised performances by the fantastic Shanghai acrobats, whose back-bending female contortionists could stack bowls on their heads with their feet while standing on their forearms, and whose male gymnasts could create tableaux of 20 figures balanced on a single circling bicycle. We admired naïve and charming peasant paintings that showed nets full of golden carp and fields of abundant harvests, with red-cheeked girls portrayed as members of the "Worker, Peasant, Soldier" proletariat. In retrospect, our romanticism was at best untutored and at worst dangerous. Nonetheless, it was the reason for my determination to learn Chinese, which I began studying in my sophomore year at Princeton, and to go to China to live.

I might have been more sensitive to signs that not everything was as rosy as I hoped, during my first visit in the summer of 1977. My organized group tour consisted of members of the U.S.–China People's Friendship Association, a populist organization intended to build people-to-people ties at a time our governments were at loggerheads. At one point, we were traveling by overnight train from Beijing to Xi'an when the guide assigned to spend two weeks with us, a kindly middle-aged lady, returned from the train platform after a ten minute stop, weeping profoundly. She was sharing a sleeping compartment with me and I asked what was wrong. She told the story of her beloved son who had been "sent down" from his home to the rural countryside to "learn from" the peasants. She had just seen him for the first time since he left home ten years earlier. She explained that the residence card system, which included everyone in China, kept him in exile. His residence card, or *hukou*, had been transferred to the countryside, keeping him trapped there; he would be unable to obtain ration coupons to buy rice, cooking oil, vegetables, clothing, and other life necessities anywhere else. She missed him terribly.

Also on that trip, an overseas Chinese woman in our group made every effort to contact her relatives and was finally allowed to glimpse them for a few moments. In the company of Party handlers, they were unable to speak freely and she was unable to discover what had happened to them during the Cultural Revolution. Their gaunt appearance and fearful demeanor made her profoundly worried.

However, instead of paying attention to these warning signals, I became more enamored than ever of a country whose people appeared strong and slim, warmly hospitable, and eager for our help. The women wore the same clothing as the men: blue or green pants and simple white shirts. They wore their hair in long braids or short bobs; they used no makeup, and indeed, there was none for sale. The men had brushy haircuts, bad teeth, and wonderfully winning smiles. The entire country seemed to rely on bicycles for transportation; automobiles were few, and reserved for "distinguished guests" like ourselves or for high-ranking Party officials. The Chinese were clearly thrilled we were visiting – everywhere we drew huge, curious, friendly crowds. Foreigners unlucky enough to be tall or to have blond or red hair were mobbed. The Chinese begged us to come back and help them to develop. Profoundly moved, I was determined to try to make a contribution.

When in early 1979 the phone call came from the Chinese Embassy telling me I had been selected to teach English in Hunan Province, I was a Masters degree student in Asian Studies at the University of

California, Berkeley. With almost six years of Chinese language training and blessed with short stature and dark hair to help me blend into local crowds, I was as well-equipped as any American might have been for the experiences that lay ahead. In retrospect, I was totally unprepared for the shocking stories I heard once I arrived and the moving events I experienced. In the course of those early two-and-a-half years of life in China, I made deep and often dangerous friendships (foreigners were still widely viewed as spies), traveled to numerous places where no foreigner had been, witnessed the struggles of a country recovering from a prolonged nightmare, and found my own writer's voice as someone who could bear witness to the suffering of a people who had no other court of appeal.

Hunan Province was Chairman Mao's home province. As a result, Maoism ran deep. Ultra-leftist military men were entrenched in power at my university, Hunan Teachers' College, and they were not at all pleased to be sent a Western foreign teacher, even if (or perhaps especially since) her English was considered an essential tool of the modernization policy of the new government. The "foreign expert" was given a large apartment, by Chinese standards, and fitted with the only air conditioner on the campus. When I turned it on, the electricity in the whole college went out – I refrained from using it. I was assigned a Party handler, a charming young woman teacher whose only duty was to spend every possible moment monitoring my activities. I fought back against her smothering attention vigorously, with eventual success. After several months she was allowed to return to her teaching assignments and instead I was placed under the charge of a genial retired army officer with a second-grade education (the military was still controlling the universities), who let me do as I pleased. I fought also for the right to ride a bicycle instead of being chauffeured in one of the only three cars in the campus garage (what if the foreigner had an accident or went somewhere off limits?) and to practice my passionate hobby, ballet, with the local song and dance troupe, who spoke of their affection for the Russian teachers who had been forced home after relations collapsed with the 1960 Sino-Soviet Split. I also fought for the right to attend the required weekly political study sessions for faculty, only to feel confused by the ill-concealed hatred that the professors displayed for the leaders, who sat in front of the room reading Party directives aloud from the official newspapers. The professors whispered loudly, knitted, spat, and showed their disdain; this was hardly what I expected.

But my political education began in earnest when I was at last permitted to teach the students. In my first months, I was considered too precious a commodity to share with anyone but the professors, many of whom were elderly former Russian teachers attempting to retool for the country's modernization drive. However, in 1977 the first examinations for university entrance had been held since before the ultra-leftist Cultural Revolution began in 1966. The students were brilliant; no professor was qualified to teach them because most English instructors had built their careers on obscure points of grammar or laborious translations of the classics (one had even achieved professorship for his translations of the poems of Chairman Mao), and at last the top students were put under my tutelage. Many of them were my age, in their mid-twenties, and had studied English in secret, often while in the countryside where they had been sent, like my former tour guide's son, to "learn from" the peasants. Such studying was highly dangerous; during the Cultural Revolution you could lose your life for listening to the Voice of America or the BBC. Yet these students, confused and embittered by the sacrifices they had made seemingly for naught, risked everything to ask questions about the outside world and about the regime under which they grew up and by which they felt misled, tricked, and exploited. They gradually started to share their stories with me, through class essays and friendships. Ironically, they often trusted me, an outsider, far more than they trusted each other, for every class had its student spies who would report what was said in order to gain their own political advancement.

From my students, I began to learn the grass roots perspective on the history of China after Mao came to power. They recalled how they were told that they were the luckiest people in the world to be born after 1949 into China's new socialist paradise. They told of the 1956–1957 Hundred Flowers Movement, a brief few months when people were encouraged to criticize the regime so as to improve it, and of the 1957 Anti-Rightist Movement which followed immediately after, when many of China's most brilliant and outspoken intellectuals, scientists, and political leaders were labeled as Rightists, silenced, imprisoned, exiled, and even executed. Although my students were children at the time, some had lost parents to politically induced divorce or persecution, and they themselves had been viewed as politically suspect as a result. They also knew about famous intellectuals, writers, and artists who were denounced as Rightists, silenced, and sent into exile in the countryside, never again to publish or resume their professional duties. They told me about the 1958–1960 Great Leap Forward, when China tried to catch up with industrialized nations through a great burst of social mobilization. Every "work unit," whether school, factory, hospital, or government institution, was organized to smelt steel in "backyard furnaces" in an effort to move China past its domineering "elder brother," the Soviet Union, and compete directly with developed Western countries in industrial output and modernization. Children and adults alike killed rats, lice, sparrows, and mosquitoes, the so-called Four Pests; farmers were induced to conduct agricultural experiments in deep plowing and close planting intended to yield one bumper harvest after the next. The "Three Hard Years" arrived immediately, from 1959 to 1961, after officials neglected the harvest, natural disasters arrived, and grain rotted in the fields. This was one of the most severe human-created famines in history, with somewhere around 30 million deaths that would not otherwise have occurred. My students told me about eating bark and gathering bitter weeds, about grandparents who starved while giving food to their children and grandchildren. Even those from big cities remembered terrible shortages. At the time, I was not attuned to the story of the deforestation that fueled the backyard furnaces, or to thinking of the great famine as a great ecological collapse, but, of course, that is what it was. Both were expressions of Mao's attempt to conquer nature.

I also heard from my students about the turmoil of the 1966–1976 Cultural Revolution. Many of them had been swept into the competitive frenzy to protect Mao against his purported enemies and joined the Red Guards, only to be manipulated into violent factional struggle against each other and against rival Red Guard groups from other universities and work units. They told of verbally and physically attacking and humiliating teachers and Party leaders, of putting up Big Character Posters drawn in large brushstrokes that enumerated the counter-revolutionary, reactionary, and revisionist crimes of the accused, of riding trains for free around the country to spread the revolution, of ritually recreating the 1934–1935 Long March by hiking arduously from one Red Army historical site to another, of humiliating religious leaders, writers, and artists for their so-called reactionary attachment to the Four Olds: old customs, culture, habits, and beliefs. They told me, too, of denouncing their own parents and siblings in an effort to be more "Red" and revolutionary than anyone else. What they did not then understand was that they were pawns in a power struggle at elite levels of political life. The protagonists included Mao's ultra-leftist radical wife Jiang Qing and her three close associates (later denounced as the Gang of Four), Mao himself, and a large cast of other central-level leaders who disagreed sharply on the political direction of the country. They also did not know that at provincial and local levels, the Cultural Revolution provided an opportunity for old rivals to settle scores. Even less were they able to reflect on their own role and responsibility for a culture of obedience, through which patronage and fealty could easily be manipulated into violent factionalism. Their impulse toward free expression, to travel throughout the country and spread revolution, and to challenge a repressive and authoritarian educational and political system, had been abused and manipulated by forces they did not understand.

Almost all of my students had been made to "volunteer" to resettle in the countryside after those few months of chaos and gratuitous violence. In early 1967, Mao sent the army into universities, middle schools, factories, and government offices in an effort to regain control, and there was nowhere to send young people when so many schools and factories were closed. Many of these "educated youth" were organized into military-style encampments and set to manual labor on China's frontiers, filling in wetlands and cutting down forests, attacking nature as they had attacked Mao's purported enemies in the Party.

During the early post-Mao years of university life, I also worked with professors who too had returned from the countryside, having been subjected to so many self-criticism sessions that they were terrified of speaking and often shielded their mouths with their hands. I met students whose only exposure to literature was from the Marxist left, whose only intellectual life had been political study in which they were made to memorize Party texts and repeat slogans. Their wicked sense of humor included using such slogans ironically in daily speech. I felt a great responsibility to provide a bridge to the world of ideas and culture. My students had never heard of Freud or the notion of the unconscious; the Beatles and Rolling Stones were unknown; the Three Mile Island nuclear meltdown was not mentioned in their newspapers when it occurred soon after my arrival in March 1979. Romantic love was still considered dangerous, if not counterrevolutionary – if a boy wrote a letter to a girl and they went for a walk together, it was tantamount to engagement and marriage. My library of foreign books, some sent ahead, some provided by the U.S. Embassy, and many cadged from generous foreign tourists, was treated as a treasure trove.

In this atmosphere, I met and eventually married a young Chinese literature student, Liang Heng. To get permission for the marriage we had to appeal to "paramount leader" Deng Xiaoping himself. As we were courting, Liang Heng narrated his life story to me systematically in Chinese and I wrote it down in English before translating it back to him orally in Chinese; this process helped him come to terms with the political upheaval that had ripped his family apart even as it helped me to understand, on a visceral level, just how traumatic the Cultural Revolution had been for the Chinese people. We later published this memoir as *Son of the Revolution*. We emigrated to the U.S. after Liang Heng received his university degree and I had been in China for three years, but we continued to return frequently to China, writing additional books about China's reforms and the changes in intellectual life. Traveling widely, we chronicled China's growing freedoms and ongoing restraints, political repression, and limits on access to information. Our adventures in remote areas closed to foreigners often involved late-night knocks on the doors of fleabag hotels where we were staying; uniformed local Public Security Bureau officials demanded to see our passports and reprimanded us for being in "closed" areas. But we evaded the serious repression experienced by democracy activists, who were sometimes sent to prison or labor camps merely for their ideas or publications, because Liang Heng was by then a U.S. citizen. China was opening up and it was often enough to apologize for being in the wrong place and continue on our way the next day. Despite such constraints, the changes under Deng Xiaoping were astounding, and by comparison to life under Mao, Chinese society under the reforms was markedly better as people's standard of living began to improve and their intense fear to abate.

Economic freedoms far outpaced political ones. In the countryside, the people's communes were disbanded and *de facto* private plots created. Systems of leasing land allowed specialized production and unleashed enterprise and innovation. In the cities, the "iron rice bowl," which guaranteed basic food and shelter for everyone in Chinese society no matter what the contribution of their labor, was "smashed." Efficiency became the order of the day as enterprises had to show they could be profitable or they were closed down. Large state-owned enterprises such as the big iron and steel mills were often exceptions, but even they were expected to create sideline businesses to stay afloat. Individual entrepreneurs began to flourish, especially among the children of high-ranking officials who often had access to commodities that were supposed to be under state control. A gray area, neither socialist nor capitalist, became a significant part of the economy, and success in life depended on connections and access to people who could help you "go through the back door" to obtain regulated or scarce goods and special permissions.

Even during the "golden decade" of increased personal freedoms from 1979 to 1989, educated Chinese spoke of a "crisis of confidence" in the Party and socialism, and some members of the central government tried to reform the political system to keep up with economic reforms. Impatient with the slow pace of change, students and intellectuals in Beijing and other cities famously demonstrated beginning in April 1989, taking over Tiananmen Square for days. It was too much, too fast. Reformist leader and Party Secretary-General Zhao Ziyang begged the students to go home, foreseeing the massacre which arrived on June 4, killing hundreds if not thousands and setting back the reform effort. Zhao ended his days under house arrest for his role in promoting political liberalization and democracy.

In the aftermath, disillusioned with the state, many bright young people turned away from politics and focused on getting ahead economically. Business and computer schools flourished, and China came into its own as the world's manufacturing hub. Getting richer, in any way possible, became a shared national passion. Apparently, the Party would be allowed to stay in power as long as the people's living standards continued to rise. The dark side of this economic activity was, of course, resource depletion and industrial pollution, the subject of this book.

Meanwhile, back in the U.S., my own career turned to the study of global environmental politics. The marriage to Liang Heng had ended and I was looking for a new direction that would bring my China experiences together with my love of nature. Fascinated by the relationship between the intellectual and personal repressions I had witnessed and the way people were despoiling the planet, I returned to China in 1999 to teach at an agricultural university in Sichuan Province and collect material and interviews for a new book, *Mao's War against Nature*, which told personal stories about how the political repression of ordinary people was mirrored in an attack against nature. State-ordered transformation of human souls was often carried out through political campaigns marshalling collective labor to "Make mountains bow their heads, make rivers flow uphill," as a Mao-era poem expressed it. Mao's uneasiness with intellectuals allowed him to dismiss the most elementary of scientific principles and celebrate his notion, as a military general, that mobilizing the country into a vast army would allow him to defeat all enemies, both human and non-human.

As this book will show, the environmental problems of the post-Mao years have only become worse, with globalized free-market capitalism an equal if not greater driver of environmental degradation than the Stalinist-style state. Perhaps the root problem is not the economic system at all: both during and after Mao, limits on public participation and freedom of information have been great obstacles to the possibility that society collectively can make wise choices. Political repression, rapid change, and the state's willingness to reorder society for its own purposes have remained constant themes which put nature under assault. But as we will discover in our exploration of China's emerging civil society, which provides more "democratic space" for individuals to voice their concerns about the condition of the environment, there are signs that an environmental movement is now emerging to help protect endangered species and clean up the pollution created by socialist and capitalist cultures alike.

I eventually became a professor of global environmental politics at the School of International Service at American University in Washington, DC, where I teach the subject, using an interdisciplinary approach, to passionate graduate and undergraduate students who wish to find solutions to our environmental crisis. This book draws upon my efforts to clarify the many scholarly and political approaches to global environmental study; it pulls them together to shine a focused light on my primary passion, China. I hope that you, the readers, will enjoy the book and that you will find it helpful, inspiring, and not overly discouraging. We need you.

Acknowledgments

This book would not have been possible without the patient persuasion of my editor at Polity Press, Louise Knight, who convinced me to write it, and David Winters, who shepherded it expertly and responsively through the publication process. Ian Tuttle copy-edited the manuscript with skill, sensitivity, and a keen eye. Many able readers were involved and I am in their debt, including Anna Brettell, Ken Conca, Mike Gelner, Gary Marcuse, and Paul Wapner, each of whom spent many hours providing detailed suggestions. Tough and helpful anonymous readers shaped the initial proposal and critiqued and improved the draft. Sikina Jinnah, Garrett Graddy, Tim Kovach, and Rong Zhu were also very helpful at critical stages. American University's School of International Service has been a wonderful base for scholarship and teaching, and I am most grateful to be here. I have learned much from my colleagues and students. I also feel extremely fortunate to have had the research assistance and editorial participation of Adam Jadhav, whose intelligent comments and questions, eye for detail, and willingness to delve deeply into the problems of a country that is not his beloved India have turned out to be one of this project's most important assets. I must also thank my ever-supportive husband Rick Shapiro, and my two cats, Binky and Scrushy, who responded to me much as they usually do, which was perhaps the greatest help of all.

Introduction: The Big Picture

1

"Climate Change Threatens China's Crops, Warns Expert."

"Amid Severe Drought, Chinese Government Admits Mistakes with Three Gorges Dam."

"China Floods: Millions Affected by Deadly Downpours."

"World's Longest Natural Gas Pipeline Goes into Operation in China."

"World's Longest Cross-sea Bridge Opens in East China."

"One in Three Buyers of Newly Built London Homes Are Chinese."

"China Expands Economic Influence around the World."

"China Suspends New High-speed Rail Projects Following Crash."

"China Closes 'Toxic' Chemical Plant after Thousands Protest."

"Company Ordered to Halt Production after Dumping Toxic Waste."

"Thousands Riot in South China over Land Grab."

These headlines, compiled from Chinese and international news feeds during just a few months in the summer and fall of 2011, reflect the breakneck changes in China's development, its global influence, and the enormity of the environmental problems that the country faces. How are we to make sense of the huge shift in China's position in the world? What does it mean for China's prospects for sustainable development? How does it affect the global environment? This book explores these questions.

China's huge environmental challenges are significant for us all. The choices the Chinese Communist Party, national government, and

Chinese people are making influence not only the health and well-being of China but the very future of the planet. Environmental issues do not stop at state borders. China's air and water pollution, dam construction, and resource consumption have a profound impact around the world. What China does affects global climate change, ozone depletion, biodiversity loss, desertification, acid rain, commodity prices, fisheries, wildlife migrations, and a host of other environmental challenges. China's expanding economy, consumption of energy, and scarcity of arable land generate environmental problems in other countries such as Canada, where the environmentally devastating Alberta tar sands are being developed with the Chinese market in mind, and Kenya, where vast areas of farmland are now owned by Chinese interests, and Myanmar (Burma), Vietnam, and Thailand, where local economies will be affected by China's construction of dams on the Salween and Mekong rivers. China's problems are interconnected with those of the rest of the planet.

China has become a major player in the international competition for resources, speeding up deforestation and land degradation around the globe. However, the huge size of China's environmental footprint is created, in part, by the export of the developed world's consumption costs: The raw materials that China extracts, not only at home but also overseas, often end up as products in stores in the developed world. The environmental degradation caused by China's resource extraction often takes place in distant countries, many in the developing world; the pollution generated during the manufacturing stage affects the Chinese people; and the finished goods are often consumed in developed countries. When consumers are finished with the products, the trash is often re-exported to the developing world as part of the illegal trade in toxic waste. The Chinese state has positioned the country for explosive economic growth, and many Chinese are growing wealthy and reaping the benefits of China becoming a global manufacturing hub; yet ordinary Chinese are bearing the brunt of global pollution, as they suffer the negative impacts of production in terms of reduced quality of life, prevalence of disease, and shortened life spans.

Here are a few striking examples of the transboundary implications of China's environmental challenges:

Particulate air pollution from China is regularly measured in California, Oregon, Washington State and Western Canada, and China is a major source of mercury deposition in the Western U.S., providing a striking reminder that a nation's environmental problems do not respect political boundaries. We know China is the source because Chinese air pollution has a high percentage of lead, and those measurements spike in Western North America in the spring when China's dust storms are most intense. The great size and intensity of these storms are caused in part by environmental mistakes made decades ago, during Mao's time, when northern grasslands were destroyed in an attempt to grow more wheat. But the sparse rainfall did not support grain production, crops died, and vast areas were reduced to desert. Now, when typhoons whip up massive dust storms over Inner Mongolia and Western China, debris can occasionally even be deposited as far away as Eastern Canada and Florida.

The dams China is building on the upper reaches of the Mekong River – in China, called the Lancang – and on the Salween River – in China, called the Nu – affect the water supply of the downriver states of Laos, Cambodia, Thailand, Vietnam, and Myanmar. Cambodians worry about the drying of lakes and the impact on fish, their primary protein source, while Vietnamese residents of the Delta are concerned about having enough water to support farming and other basic livelihoods. This dam-building activity is complicated by the fact that China (like Myanmar) is not a full member or treaty signatory but only a dialogue partner in the well-established Mekong River Commission; it is thus less likely to be bound by collective decisions. Upstream dam-building plans and activities in China on the rivers originating in the Tibetan Plateau and elsewhere in Western China could also threaten the water supplies of people in India, Nepal, Pakistan, Bangladesh, and Kazakstan; indeed, as we see from this list, there are tensions over transboundary watercourses between China and almost all of its territorial neighbors.

The Chinese people's growing appetite for exotic meats, animal parts, and plants threatens rare and endangered species; Chinese gastronomic and medical traditions see consuming a species as a way of acquiring desirable characteristics like strength, prowess, and longevity. The Chinese demand for body parts of rhinoceroses, tigers, bears, pangolins, and turtles, to name just a few creatures under siege, is felt in many other Asian countries and indeed throughout the world. Even in North America, American black bears are poached for their gall bladders, and wild plants like American ginseng root are poached from parks and protected areas and smuggled to the Chinese medicinal market. Sharks, whose fins are sliced off to make soup, are in decline throughout the world and captured from as far away as the Galapagos.

Since the 1998 Yangzi River floods, when China banned logging in the headwaters of its major rivers, China's import of exotic hardwoods from Indonesia, Myanmar, Cambodia, and other remaining tropical forests has increased dramatically. The ban increased pressure on some of the world's last remaining old growth forests, in part to feed a market in furniture exported to the U.S. and other developed countries. China is in a dominant position in the middle of the commodity chain between loggers and consumers. Without more active participation from China, efforts to create "sustainable" forest product certifications are doomed to fail. The logging ban in China has also had an enormous effect on the forests of the Russian Far East, the last redoubt of the Siberian Tiger, and as far away as Canada, where the logging industry is enjoying a recovery thanks to its major new customer.

China has overtaken the U.S. as the world's largest emitter of carbon dioxide (CO_2) and other greenhouse gasses. Together with other developing countries, China argues that its "survival emissions" should not be compared to the "luxury emissions" of developed countries, which have enjoyed the benefits of burning fossil fuels that put most of the carbon into the atmosphere and should rightfully bear the primary costs of saving the global atmospheric infrastructure which sustains life. This position affects the outcome of the ongoing global climate change negotiations to extend or replace the 1997 Kyoto Protocol, which have so far met with failure. However, even in per capita terms China's emissions are rising dramatically, and pressure is mounting on China to modify its position that it should be treated as a developing country. Encouragingly, China is taking unilateral steps to reduce emissions intensity and increase the percentage of renewable resources in its energy mix.

The rising middle class in China, as in India and other rapidly developing countries, is using more refrigerants and air conditioners, reversing some of the favorable movement toward repairing the thinning stratospheric ozone layer which protects the Earth from ultraviolet radiation. China, like other less-developed countries which signed the 1987 Montreal Protocol, had more time than developed ones to phase out ozone-depleting substances like CFCs (technically named chlorofluorocarbons and marketed as Freon), halons, and the agricultural fumigant methyl bromide, which is still used on strawberries and other crops. Although the phase-out period is over, CFC substitutes such as hydrofluorocarbons (HFCs) and hydrochlorofluorocarbons (HCFCs) are also ozone-depleting, if less so. Even in the best case scenario, increased demand for such products in the developing world may undermine the world's most successful example of international cooperation on environmental issues.

Acid rain deposition from sulfur dioxide (SO_2) emissions, to which China is a major contributor, has destroyed forests in Japan and Korea. This remains a sore point in diplomatic relations in Northeast Asia, with as much as half of the acid rain in the region coming from China's coal-fired power plants and automobile exhaust.

In a competition over the power to exploit natural resources, the Chinese are asserting territorial maritime claims over the Spratly and Paracel Islands in the South China Sea. There, multiple actors including Vietnam, the Philippines, Malaysia, Brunei and Taiwan also assert rights to oil and natural gas sea-beds, fisheries, and shipping lanes. Fragile relationships in that region are unstable, and the United States' support for its traditional allies has created friction in the relationship between the U.S. and China.

Chinese international investment in oil, gas, and minerals, welcome as it may be to political elites overseas, fuels environmentally destructive extractive activities in places as far flung as Central Asia, Ecuador, Sudan, and Iran. Chinese foreign aid programs often facilitate such extraction by carving roads into wilderness and across deserts, bringing development into fragile ecosystems and contributing to the current great wave of global species extinctions.

As fascinating and sobering as these examples may be, they cannot be understood fully without appreciating China's domestic political pressures, struggles, history, and culture. Thus, the primary focus of this book is on the domestic roots of some of these transnational challenges, for it is within China that much of the future of the planet will be decided. Conventional "realist" political analysis tends to see nation-states as unitary, power-seeking actors in an anarchic world and do not uncover the complexity of China's political and social landscape. We need to recognize the multiplicity of actors who play a role in China's future and appreciate the country's geographic variety, regional disparities, and ethnic and cultural complexity, as well as the unique character of China's authoritarian political system, with its economic and social freedoms and contradictions. All of these factors will play a role in determining China's future environmental "footprint" and transnational impacts. What are the implications of the fact that, as Joseph

Kahn and Jim Yardley expressed it in an extensive 2007 *New York Times* series on China's environment, China is "Choking on Growth"? How will the Chinese navigate the challenges they are facing, and what dynamics affect their choices?

Before we begin to approach these enormous questions, here are just a few facts to illustrate the severity of China's environmental crisis. The World Bank has found that 20 of the world's 30 most polluted cities are in China, primarily because of heavy coal use, with Shanxi Province's coal mining city Linfen the dirtiest. China's high economic growth rate – close to 10 percent per year between 2000 and 2011 – must be greatly discounted with the inclusion of environmental costs in lost work days, premature deaths, and pollution clean-up. In 2004, for example, economic losses caused by environmental pollution accounted for as much as 3 percent of GDP. Additional costs resulting from resources depletion and ecological damage could not be calculated due to lack of data (State Environmental Protection Administration 2006). Efforts by some government officials and think tank scholars to create a reliable "Green Gross Domestic Product" calculation for China stalled from 2004 onwards, in part because of the political sensitivity of the effort and the difficulty of obtaining reliable statistics.

Air pollution is a huge challenge. The problem was made famous by the attention to poor air quality in the capital during the lead-up to the 2008 Beijing Olympics, but it is even more serious in other parts of the country. The World Resources Institute (1999) found that total suspended particulates (TSP) and SO_2, both produced by burning coal, far exceed World Health Organization guidelines in the majority of Chinese cities. Lung diseases such as tuberculosis and cancer are so prevalent that Chinese "cancer villages," in which cancer death rates due to air and water pollution are far above the national average, are well documented. By 2010, the media and Internet had drawn attention to 459 cancer villages distributed across 29 of China's 31 provinces (Liu 2010).

Meanwhile, severe water pollution affects 75 percent of China's rivers and lakes and 90 percent of urban groundwater, with 28 percent of China's rivers ranked category five (the worst) on a Chinese scale of one to five, so toxic that they are unsuitable even for agricultural use. China's major lakes such as Lake Tai in Eastern China and Dianchi in Yunnan are ranked at category five (Chinese Academy of Social Sciences 2008). A 2007 OECD study found that hundreds of millions of Chinese people drink water contaminated by arsenic, fluoride, untreated wastewater, fertilizers and pesticides.

In addition to pollution problems, groundwater aquifers are rapidly being depleted as users dig deeper wells each year. Falling water tables in North China threaten the water supply of Beijing. The great Yellow River does not reliably flow all the way to the sea; in 1997, the worst year so far, it failed to reach the eastern delta for 226 days, essentially drying out. In a book originally published in Chinese in 1999, water pollution activist Ma Jun states that 400 out of 600 cities are facing water shortages, including 30 out of the 32 largest cities (2004). Attempting to deal with this threat, the Chinese government is building a three-channel "South–North Water Transfer Project" [*nanshui beidiao* 南水北调] to move water from the Yangzi to the Yellow River, a multi-billion dollar megaproject with enormous environmental and social implications, including effects on irrigation in the South where farmers accustomed to access will be deprived, human rights implications for the forcibly relocated, and devastating ecological impacts on the Tibetan Plateau should the Westernmost channel be built (International Rivers Network n.d., a).

Research studies have suggested that water stress could create massive numbers of dislocated "environmental refugees" in coming decades as large parts of China face water shortages (Shalizi 2006). The World Bank has estimated that more than 300 million people in rural China lack access to safe drinking water (Xie 2009). Water shortages, sea-level rise, increased droughts, and disruptions of rainfall patterns from climate change could cause the displacement of millions of Chinese by 2050 (Myers 1997). China's rainfall is already highly seasonal – with 70 percent falling during the rainy months and 30 percent during the dry – and geographically uneven. The North, with 60 percent of China's cropland, has only 16 percent of its water, while the South, with 40 percent of the cropland, has 84 percent (Loh 2011). When climate change, pollution, and overuse for irrigation and industry are added to this fundamentally insecure situation, the Chinese people's access to water becomes highly unpredictable.

Given the severity of these and other entrenched problems such as deforestation, erosion, desertification, heavy metal pollution, salinization, loss of arable land, acid rain, and biodiversity loss, China's handling of its environmental crisis has become of critical importance to the country's stability and the legitimacy of the government. Indeed, the nation's environmental challenges are so severe and so central to the manner in which China will "rise" that it is no exaggeration to say that they cannot be separated from its national identity and the government's ability to provide for the Chinese people. Acute environmental degradation threatens social stability; increasingly, environmental protests trigger state concerns about broader unrest. "Environmental mass incidents" [*huanjing quntixing shijian* 环境群体性事件] sparked by local pollution are estimated to number 5,000 per year (Ma, Tianjie 2008/2009), with some reports putting the figure much higher. Many of these involve only a small crowd or short protest and are resolved in a matter of hours, while others involve thousands of people and shut down major cities.

The Chinese Communist Party and the state government's controls of power are at stake as they try to achieve contradictory aims. They must provide an improvement in material living standards in a country whose hinterlands are still desperately poor and whose middle class is just beginning to discover the joys of consumption after decades of privation. At the same time, they must deal with industrial accidents, the environmental costs of the country's manufacturing so many of the world's consumer products, and growing resistance to toxic pollution. Despite being armed with some of the world's best environmental laws and regulations, China's bureaucracy faces huge challenges in implementation. Local incentives to cut corners on regulatory implementation and enforcement and pursue polluting practices prevail. While some government officials and agencies are making serious attempts to shift the country to an alternative development model, these efforts often seem puny when pitted against powerful forces of corruption, decentralized authority structures beyond the reach of the law, and incentives to focus on economic growth to the exclusion of other considerations. China's civil society is still weak and mistrusted by central powers, so efforts to deal with severe environmental problems "from the bottom" through public pressure are also inadequate in the face of monumental problems. When, moreover, one considers that there are cultural factors that emphasize conspicuous consumption and mistrust of government authority, and even rationalize illegal behavior in the interest of financial gain, the challenges can seem very great indeed. As Jonathan Watts writes in *When a Billion Chinese Jump*, "China's political system now exhibits the worst elements of dictatorship and democracy: power lies neither at the top nor the bottom, but within a middle class of developers, polluters, and local officials who are difficult to regulate, monitor, and challenge" (2010b, p. 290).

China's environmental challenges are thus tied to domestic political structures, rapid economic growth, and an intense phase of globalization in which the entire planet is involved. We can productively use the lens of development studies to understand these dynamics, since China has so rapidly moved from being a less developed country to a transitional one to one that is already a superpower. The key question is whether this unprecedented development will be "sustainable."

The term sustainable development was articulated in 1987 in the United Nations World Commission on Environment and Development's report, *Our Common Future* (also known as the Brundtland Report) and is commonly defined as meeting the needs of present generations without endangering the ability of future generations to do the same (WCED 1987). In the Chinese context, the question can be phrased: Can Chinese people alive today pursue healthy and meaningful lives without stealing resources from their children or from vulnerable populations within the country and abroad? The sustainable development lens suggests other difficult ethical questions inherent in China's rise: Do the Chinese people have an inherent right to the higher living standards enjoyed in the developed world? Are such standards even possible? To what extent are China's environmental problems due to the rest of the world's consumption patterns? Can Chinese cities improve their environments without shifting pollution to other, more vulnerable regions? Can China deal with the acute poverty in much of the country's Far West, even as eastern parts of the nation grow richer? What is the cultural and historical context in which China is trying to achieve sustainable development, should it be embraced or rejected in the search for success? Finally, in a world of increasing limits on resources and pollution "sinks," or repositories, is it even possible to build an equitable world in which people enjoy equal access to resources without taking them from successive generations, from the vulnerable, or from other species? While these questions do not have definitive answers, they are well worth considering as members of the international community concerned about the planet's dire environmental situation seek to build alliances and craft solutions to collective challenges.

Five core analytical concepts can bring China's choices and prospects into relief: the implications of *globalization*, or the increasingly complex and powerful ties that bind China and the rest of the world; the challenges of *governance*, which expands the notion of what the government can and cannot do and of the reach of the state; contested *national identity*, where competing world views and value systems offer different interpretations of China's past, present, and future; evolution of *civil society*, which helps us focus on the complex relationship between citizens' groups and power; and problems of *environmental justice* and equity, which involve the displacement of environmental harm across time and space. These concepts are doubtless familiar to students and scholars of international relations, and each one will be explored more deeply in the chapters that follow, but it will be helpful to introduce them briefly here so as to explain how they will be used in this volume.

GLOBALIZATION

For the purposes of this book, globalization can usefully be considered as a shrinkage of time and space due to the introduction and spread of technologies such as the Internet and air travel, and as an increase in the flow of goods, capital, people, and ideas across borders (Mittelman 2000). The interdependence of nations in the global economy continues to increase and grow more complex, while the pace of change in China's status and influence within that global trend is unprecedented. The flow of globalization extends in multiple directions, both out and in, like a complex web; China's economy has become so intertwined with the economies of the rest of the world that a shift in China's situation can almost immediately be felt elsewhere, and a shift elsewhere can almost immediately be felt in China.

For example, drought which leads China to seek more grain on the world market raises global food prices, pushing marginalized people elsewhere in the world toward desperation. China's monetary policies affect the balance of trade with the U.S. and other major powers, and hence the volume and intensity of the flow of manufactured products. The U.S. debt crisis of 2011 infuriated Chinese investors, who questioned their government's willingness to purchase so many U.S. Treasury bonds; yet in effect China lends the U.S. government money to sustain its economy so that American consumers can purchase Chinese products. China's newfound ability to purchase real estate overseas and invest in multinational companies alters landscapes, both literally and figuratively. Massive foreign investment in China, both direct and through joint ventures, drives resource extraction and pollution. In sum, globalization, and China's interconnectedness with the world, explains many changes in China's environmental situation, both positive and negative.

The enormity of the change in China's situation vis-à-vis the rest of the world may become clearer if we compare the late 1970s just after the death of Mao Zedong, when China was still largely isolated from the world, to today. A few of my personal recollections about the flow of goods, capital, people and ideas from the early days of the reforms may underscore the transformation China has experienced during these few short decades.

Goods

Immediately after the death of Mao in 1976, Chinese people were so afraid of being called capitalists that they hesitated to sell even a few vegetables. When the first few peasants began to gather at the gate of the college where I worked, offering a few bunches of spinach or a basket of eggs, the professors commented nervously on this dangerous "free market" [*ziyou shichang* 自由市场]. Both intellectuals and farmers had been severely criticized for capitalist leanings during the Cultural Revolution, some even "persecuted to death," as the Chinese phrase puts it, driven to severe ill-health or suicide. During the first few years of Communist Party Secretary Deng Xiaoping's post-Mao economic reforms, which allowed groups and even individuals to form profit-making enterprises and forced state-owned enterprises to be responsible for their own profits and losses, the government felt obliged to introduce a propaganda campaign to reassure the Chinese people that the days of being persecuted for accumulating wealth were over. The slogan went: "It's glorious to get rich" [*zhifu guangrong* 致富光荣]. Today, of course, China is the manufacturing hub of the world, as we discover easily when we look at the labels on our clothing, toys, and electronic equipment. When in March 2011 *Forbes* calculated the net worth of the world's billionaires, 115 on the list were from China, second in number only to the U.S. and nearly double the number of the year before. Three Chinese energy companies took spots numbers five, six, and seven in *Fortune* magazine's Global 500 list of the largest companies in 2011. Much of this industrial activity involved heavy pollution to produce goods for the global market.

Capital

The handful of Chinese who were able to visit the outside world during the late 1970s generally did so through organized exchange visits. They had little or no foreign currency to spend, for the *renminbi* (or *yuan*) was not freely convertible. In the early 1980s, on a short contract as a Mandarin interpreter for a group of government officials visiting the U.S., I was amused and somewhat saddened to see them collect ashtrays and soap from American hotel rooms, their only way of satisfying the enormous expectations of a gift-giving culture. Today, so powerful have Chinese government investments become that as of September 2011, the U.S. Treasury Department indicates, mainland China held 1.17 trillion dollars in U.S. public debt. This staggering sum illustrates the change in China's fortunes and underlines how interdependent the global economy has become. The environmental implications of China's newfound buying power are enormous: To satisfy insecurities about supply of key resources, from grain to minerals to fossil fuels, the

Chinese are buying land and influence, sometimes in developed places like Vancouver, sometimes in places rich in fossil fuels and other resources like Nigeria and Ecuador. Sometimes they do so through outright purchase, sometimes through investment. Another example of the power of Chinese capital is through foreign aid programs that have persuaded the holdout countries who recognized Taiwan as the legitimate government of China to change allegiances (among them Costa Rica, which received in thanks a fabulous 35,000 seat sports arena which opened in March 2011). Capital flows both ways: Foreign direct investment (FDI) by multinational corporations, tied to global trade, is now a significant part of the Chinese economy; in 2010, reported foreign investment in China was $105.7 billion (Ministry of Commerce 2011).

People

The enormity of the change in the flow of people becomes clear when one considers that, immediately after Mao's death in 1976, the handful of foreigners who could get visas to visit China could reliably find each other in the lobby of the Beijing Hotel or changing planes in Tokyo's Narita airport. Ordinary Chinese simply could not get a passport to travel abroad; my Hunan Teachers' College English-language students expected to spend their lives mastering and eventually teaching a language they would never use overseas and perhaps rarely employ to communicate with a native speaker. In 2010, the Chinese Ministry of Education counted almost a quarter of a million foreign students in China, and in 2011, more than 1.2 million were studying overseas. Statistics from the Chinese Ministry of Human Resources and Labor Security, published in 2011 by the state-run news agency *Xinhua*, showed 231,700 foreigners working in China in 2010, up slightly from the year before. Millions of Chinese now regularly travel abroad and the number is growing rapidly. In fiscal year 2010, according to U.S.

Department of State figures, more than 30,000 Chinese born on the mainland were given immigrant visas, and more than 653,000 non-immigrant visas were issued from the five U.S. consular posts in China. So attractive has the Chinese job market become for Westerners facing bleak employment prospects at home that some are even focusing their job searches there.

The flow of people facilitates the flow of ideas, in both directions – the Chinese government is actively making it more attractive for foreigners to study in China as part of a "soft power" strategy to spread its influence through diplomacy and exchange. At the same time it is finding it difficult to control the impact of foreign ideas, as was seen quite dramatically and notoriously in Beijing during the U.N.'s 1995 Fourth World Conference on Women, where non-governmental organizations (NGOs) were relegated to a location outside of Beijing but nevertheless managed to express a vibrant level of civil society participation that left Chinese officials scrambling to try to exert control. Cell phones and social networking technologies like *weibo*, the Chinese equivalent of Twitter, and personal blogs have challenged state-run media. The 2011 Arab Spring in Egypt and elsewhere in the Middle East led the government to intensify efforts to control Internet information and to censor references to a potential copycat "Jasmine Revolution," using filters to cut communication in which the word jasmine appeared (and causing headaches for buyers and sellers of tea and perfume).

Ideas

During the Mao years, the handful of approved foreign writers included only the left-wing: Balzac, Tolstoy, Twain, London, and Dickens. I vividly remember how people lined up for hours when the first post-Cultural Revolution Western film, "The Sound of Music," was released for viewing in China. The Chinese had literally been cut off from the outside world; at the height of ultra-left extremism, even communicating with overseas relatives could mean death. After Mao died and the Four Modernizations (in agriculture, industry, defense, and science and technology) became national policy and were deemed to necessitate training in the English language, I became employed as the only foreign teacher at my university, the first since a Russian language teacher had been expelled in 1960 after the Sino-Soviet split. The responsibility for providing a bridge to so much missing information felt very great. Nowadays, the universities of Peking, Qinghua, Fudan and elsewhere rival the world's best, and foreign teachers and students are so numerous as to merit barely a glance. Even small provincial universities and technical institutes have English language and sometimes specific subject instructors from overseas.

While the flow of goods and capital provides much of the impetus for China's environmental problems, the flow of people and ideas also provides mitigating possibilities. Importantly for the subject of this book, environmental information flows relatively freely from the outside world, with even blocked websites available to Chinese who know how to circumvent China's Internet firewalls. The Chinese effort to understand how best to navigate their environmental crisis is reflected in increasing transparency of data about the impacts of pollution, climate change, and ozone depletion, as well as about the tactics and strategies of environmental non-governmental groups. Chinese government officials have long been major players in global environmental negotiations, and now Chinese citizens' groups are starting to participate as well. Foreign values like government and corporate accountability and rule of law have also become goals for China, nurtured in part through extensive exchanges of legal professionals and intensive domestic debate among Chinese intellectuals and policy makers. Alternative energy technologies like solar, wind, and biomass have not only been widely adopted but are undergoing intense research and development, and China has even become the world's leading exporter of solar panels, where manufacturers see tremendous opportunity for growth. Excitement over the creation of green jobs through a new green economy is growing (Pan et al. 2011). On the less positive side, Western-style consumption is portrayed and often distorted in films and other media, modeling lavish lifestyles and wasteful resource use that does not promote sustainability.

GOVERNANCE

The concept of governance, with its Latin root in "steering," broadens the study of politics beyond that of the state, with its laws, regulations, and "monopoly on the legitimate use of violence," as Max Weber so famously expressed it, to focus on the processes, policies, laws, and institutions that affect social relations and guide public attitudes and behavior. In the case of China, using this broader understanding helps us see the complexity and limitations of the government's efforts to implement environmental laws and regulations, to ensure a safer food supply, and to crack down on intellectual property violations. Environmentalists use the term "global governance" to draw attention to collective efforts to address transnational problems that states alone cannot solve, such as climate change, ozone depletion, overfishing, and threats to migratory and endangered species, especially given the international state system's relative absence of meaningfully enforceable or "hard" international law. Non-governmental forces and actors such as citizens' groups also participate in "steering" societies and shaping public behavior, often circumventing the state entirely. In thinking about governance, we may also find useful Michel Foucault's concept of "governmentality," which shifts attention from the state's power over death to its power over the ways that its citizens live. This is a useful concept for understanding authoritarian countries that seek to regulate important aspects of their citizens' lives, including customs and social structures that affect behavior and attitudes toward natural resources. For China this is particularly relevant in border areas, where traditional nomadic societies are being forced to give up their old ways, often in the name of environmental protection.

NATIONAL IDENTITY

The Chinese people's struggles to define their national identity also provide us with important insights into China's environmental challenges. Every nation tells itself stories of where it has been and where it is going, thereby providing citizens with a shared understanding of the past and sense of the future. The stories are supported by myths, legends, and official renditions of national history; they are taught by families and schools and reinforced through national symbols such as the images on currency, flags, and statues. They are enacted and brought to life through rituals such as graduations, sporting events, religious ceremonies, and holiday traditions. The concept of national identity captures not only these stories but also people's value systems and world views, as well as ingrained cultural traits such as attitudes toward authority, the importance of the collective versus the individual, and understandings of what makes one people different from another. It captures perceptions of nature, the outdoors, and the relationship between people and animals. In the Chinese case, the concept also captures a competing self-understanding of the Chinese nation as both superior and inferior to others, the formerly great Middle Kingdom more recently humiliated by foreign imperialist powers, beginning with the great age of colonization. The national sensitivity over rank and respect is undergirded and reinforced by a Confucian philosophy that sees harmonious societies as inherently hierarchical and emphasizes the importance of "face," or respect, in dealings with others; the correct performance of one's assigned social role within a network of personal connections is one of the highest cultural values, and demonstrating respect for one's superiors by "giving face" is a primary lubricant for good social and political relationships.

As this book will argue, the preoccupation with reasserting China's rightful place of respect in the world underlies many of China's development decisions and helps us to understand the important role of national identity in China's prospects for achieving sustainable development. In its search for national greatness and improved living standards for more than a billion people, will China pursue the same level of wasteful consumption that Western powers have enjoyed and, if so, can the planet afford that? Or is there a possibility that by "leapfrogging," using clean technologies, better forms of social organization focused on local communities, creating sustainable cities and clean transportation networks, and reviving agricultural systems that maintain the connection between farmer and consumer even in modern cities, China can show the world a gentler, less destructive way of achieving high living standards and human development? Is there a possibility of reshaping national identity and the historical narrative in such a way that it promotes values of moderation, humility, and gentleness, or will "face" and conspicuous consumption continue to govern Chinese actions at home and abroad? These are core questions both for the Chinese people and for the world. Many Chinese are plumbing their traditions for guidance, but for a Chinese style of environmentalism to gain broad acceptance, it will need to address national pride and the thirst for global leadership, power, and respect.

CIVIL SOCIETY

A concept closely related to governance is that of civil society, which can be understood as that space in society that exists between the level of the individual (or family, as some define it) and the state, where citizens come together "horizontally" and freely for shared purposes. Civil society can include advocacy groups such as Greenpeace or the

International Fund for Animal Welfare, hobbyist clubs such as callig-raphers and practitioners of tai chi (*taijiquan*), charitable organizations such as Wheelchair Foundation China, academic establishments such as universities and cram schools, religious institutions such as temples, mosques, and churches, as well as "illegal" groups such as practitioners of Falungong. As the Italian political theorist Antonio Gramsci pointed out in his *Prison Notebooks*, written in the 1930s but still relevant for understanding contemporary societies, civil society is often "penetrated" by the state; the relationship is complex and often contested and ambivalent (Gramsci 1991). The state and its institutions use civil society groups to try to mould people into useful citizens, even as civil society groups attempt to influence and mould the state. Government-run schools teach approved curricula and reward certain behavior and types of learning through grades and examinations; families and reli-gious institutions "socialize" us and teach us how to behave in ways that will allow us to succeed in the society into which we were born. In China, this relationship is particularly uneasy and the state works especially hard to control citizens' groups, including environmental non-governmental organizations (ENGOs), by requiring them to reg-ister and by monitoring their activities. At times the state refuses to recognize new groups, or even dissolves existing ones. However, the rising demands of the middle class for cleaner air and water, informa-tion transparency, and government accountability are important impe-tuses for a more articulate and powerful civil society, albeit one with "Chinese characteristics" of collaboration with friendly government forces.

ENVIRONMENTAL JUSTICE AND THE DISPLACEMENT OF ENVIRONMENTAL HARM

An important measurement used by those who study environmental politics is that of the environmental footprint. Individuals can take a simple online footprint quiz to calculate their impact on the planet; schools and universities, corporations, towns, cities, and nations can use more sophisticated measures to calculate their sustainability index in order to create a baseline for improvement or to track changes in energy consumption, carbon usage, or other behavior they hope to improve. A footprint can even serve as a way of measuring a positive contribution, as when users of solar power send electricity back into the grid. Indeed, the concept of the carbon footprint underlies international negotiations on climate change, as each country agrees to strive toward a greenhouse gas emissions limit that it believes it can achieve without suffering devastating economic damage. Yet the calculation of the footprint of an individual, institution, or country often overlooks what Peter Dauvergne (1997) and others have called its "shadow ecology." From where does it extract the resources it consumes? To where does it export its waste? What are the hidden costs of daily choices?

The final theme that will teach us about the underlying dynamics of China's environmental challenges is that of the displacement of environmental harm, which is a close cousin to the concept of environmental justice. Powerful regions and states tend to displace destructive extractive activities and to shift toxic wastes to weaker or poorer communities, regions, and countries. They do so not necessarily out of malice; such dynamics are often cost-effective and driven by the market, and other factors such as investment incentives and access to raw materials also influence the movement of businesses around the world. Nonetheless, advocates for environmental justice have documented this relocation of harm as a common phenomenon at both transnational and domestic levels: Weak communities, regions, and states bear a disproportionate burden of the costs of economic activity, while wealthy ones enjoy most of the benefits. Immanuel Wallerstein (1979) has articulated a world systems theory describing a dynamic among "core, semi-periphery, and periphery" which may help explicate this process: Marginalized areas tend to enrich stronger ones through a process that shifts wealth. In the Chinese case, the "core" may generally be understood as the wealthy areas on the Eastern coast, while the periphery is the poor Western interior. We can also see this phenomenon at work within provinces, as industries gravitate to less developed areas within regions or outside the city limits, often with the government in developed areas pressing for industrial restructuring or clean-up, while local leaders in poor regions offer incentives in an effort to alleviate poverty and provide economic opportunities.

China's thirst for resources, from timber and wildlife to fossil fuels and minerals, has led to an increase in environmental degradation in places beyond its national boundaries, contributing to forests denuded of timber as far away as Liberia and to mountains gutted of coal as far away as Australia. At the same time, but less frequently noted in the Western media which so often demonize China, developed country consumers have displaced many of the costs and benefits of manufacturing onto China and the Chinese people. By using the analytical lenses of environmental justice and displacement of environmental harm, we can more clearly understand that within China, as among states, there are winners and losers. We can try to avoid easy finger-pointing and appreciate more fully a core dynamic that underlies resource extraction and pollution throughout the world.

ACADEMIC DISCIPLINES AND THE STUDY OF ENVIRONMENTAL CHALLENGES

We conclude this introductory chapter with some reflections on how various academic disciplines approach environmental problems, as this may help readers to frame their own interests and articulate ideas for research projects. The most conventional way is by country study: The problems of Indonesia, or South Africa, or Myanmar, or of course China are the subject of numerous policy briefs, planning documents, scholarly studies, and term papers. One could also conduct a comparative study of two or more countries by issue area – China as compared with India on sustainable energy policy, for example, or the U.S. as compared with the E.U. on climate change, or Costa Rica's protected areas as compared with those of China. Of course, this country-level approach is severely limited by the fact that environmental issues transcend political borders. Although national policy and response must be understood, environmental problems do not carry passports, and eco-regions rarely correspond to nation-states.

Another important way of approaching environmental issues is to focus on sectors – water, energy, grasslands, wildlife, mining, agriculture, air – using a "resources" approach, which tends to emphasize the utility of these sectors for human beings. Or, we can become even more specific: We can focus on lakes, or on an individual lake such as Dianchi in Yunnan or Lake Tai in Eastern China, where clean-up efforts have been extensive but to date have failed; or on rivers in general or on a specific river such as the Yangzi, Yellow, Pearl, Jinsha, or Nu. We can focus on a specific energy policy, such as China's efforts in the solar power market, or nuclear, focusing on China's ambitious plans to build many nuclear power plants. We can focus on hydropower dams, or on a specific dam such as the highly controversial Three Gorges Dam or the Zipingpu Dam, which narrowly missed collapse during the 2008 Sichuan earthquake and which some seismologists think might have contributed to the quake by shifting weight near a fault line. We can focus on a specific mineral such as coal, copper, zinc, or the "rare earths," which are used for defense, circuit boards, and solar panels, of which China produces more than 90 percent of global supplies. (China's withdrawal of rare earth export licenses for sale to Japan in 2010 was seen as a way to pressure its old rival over disputed islands in the East China Sea, and its control of the minerals has caused energy-efficient light bulb costs to skyrocket in the U.S.) We can focus on threats to a specific species, such as the beautiful and delicate Yangzi River dolphin which, sadly, is now gone forever, the only dolphin driven to extinction by human pollution and the noise of ships interfering with its communication abilities. Or we can study the plight of the Giant Panda, where conservation efforts reveal diverging philosophies, with some Chinese scientists focusing on captive breeding or even cloning, as compared to Western (and some Chinese) scientists emphasizing habitat conservation. We can focus on a specific event such as one of those listed in the next chapter – a specific oil spill, a specific earthquake, a specific sporting event. We can organize our investigations according to key concepts, as we are doing in this book – globalization, governance, national identity, civil society, environmental justice. Or we can focus on an intransigent environmental problem such as the trade in wildlife and its relationship to traditional Chinese medicine, which understands food as a form of medicine and which considers all living creatures as potentially edible; or on illegal logging, using a commodity chain analysis which illuminates timber's dark journey; or on e-waste and its sources and impacts. Any of these issues could provide material for an entire book.

Let us also take a moment to consider the various scholarly disciplines and see what each might contribute in terms of interpretation and analysis. Scholars from all fields have become concerned about our planet's environmental crisis, and they have tried to use their theories, tools, and assumptions to consider the root causes of, and potential solutions to, environmental woes. In simplified form, here is a taste of how some of the disciplines might contribute to our understanding of China's environmental challenges.

Within the fields of political science and international relations, which tend to focus on the distribution and exertion of power, a range of schools of thought about global environmental politics is relevant for the study of Chinese environmental issues. "Neoliberal institutionalists" emphasize states' shared interests and study the organizations, treaties, declarations, and legal frameworks that contribute to the international governance of transboundary problems, focusing on bilateral, regional, and global cooperation on environmental issues and trying to see how such institutions can be strengthened. For China, such scholars often analyze China's role in negotiations and participation in treaties and agreements. "Realists," however, often discredit these efforts to create global governance institutions as ineffective. They see the global state system as a zero-sum game, and tend toward a cynical view of the prospects that any of the great powers, including China, will curb their global quests for resources or create an equitable system of sharing resources. By contrast, international relations "constructivists" focus on the importance of ideas and emphasize the role of scientific discoveries about climate change and ozone depletion, the political power of consensus groups like the Intergovernmental Panel on Climate Change and the International Union for the Conservation of Nature, and the evolving roles of global civil society and the media in creating pressure points for change. For them, how state power is projected is "socially constructed" and amenable to influence by framing, shaming, and other socialization techniques. Finally, "international political economists" focus on the role of global trade networks and regulations, the flow of goods and materials across borders, the direction of such flows (usually from developing countries to developed ones), and the movement of capital and role of corporations and multilateral development lending institutions like the World Bank. These varied approaches draw our attention to questions such as the nature of power in the modern world, the changeability of state interests, and the effectiveness of international institutional and legal arrangements. They also indicate different pathways into creating social change.

Other disciplines also have much to contribute to this conversation. Environmental anthropologists focus on the importance of culture, often through the subfield of religion and ecology. This lens is useful for looking at the intransigence of traditional beliefs such as the power of taking medicine containing powdered tiger bones, for example, or at Confucianism's focus on the utility of nature as compared with Buddhism's reverence for life (and reincarnation) or Daoism's emphasis on adapting to nature or going with its flow. An important field within human geography is political ecology, which focuses on how unequal power relationships among human beings affect land use and cause environmental degradation (Blaikie 1985). Similarly, sociologists, who often focus on the roles of race, class, and gender in social structure, have pioneered the subfields of environmental justice and social ecology, which argue that the human domination of nature is related to human domination of other humans (Bookchin 1980). For them, environmental degradation is essentially a product of inequality and injustice in the human world; we see their influence in concepts such as displacement of environmental harm. Meanwhile, environmental historians remind us that environmental degradation in China has been occurring for millennia, and they often use counterfactual reasoning to explain how events turned out as they did. Tigers might have survived in Southeast China, for example, if not for the deforestation which caused them to lose their habitat (Marks 2006). Environmental economists seek to measure the real costs of resource exploitation and degradation by assigning monetary value to goods formerly considered "free," such as publicly held forests and the atmosphere (considered part of the global commons), and they try to create "green" accounting systems that measure "ecosystem services" such as water purification by wetlands and pollination by bees; in China, environmental economists have engaged in this effort and found it challenging because of the unreliability of Chinese statistics and the political sensitivity of the project. By contrast, ecological economists reject growth-oriented public policy as unsustainable and argue that we need to create a system that would create what Herman Daly (1996) has called a "steady state economy," or development without growth. This notion is related to the architect's notion of building a cradle-to-cradle economy rather than the cradle-to-grave system that currently drives economic transactions, such that all material goods can be reused indefinitely (McDonough and Braungart 2002).

These lenses on our subject produce fruitful insights, and we will be using a multidisciplinary approach in the pages ahead. Yet our chosen concepts will be most useful for organizing the subject at hand. Globalization, governance, national identity, civil society, and environmental justice derive primarily from political theory, anthropology, and political ecology, fields which I, the author, find to have compelling explanatory power. These concepts are far from exhaustive. Readers are encouraged to find their way more deeply into the issues raised in these pages through the approaches that most resonate for them, whether they are quantitative or qualitative, macro or micro, synchronic or diachronic, oriented toward international or national policy and law, or toward grassroots organizations or problems. Readers are also encouraged to read widely. Enjoyable first-person journalistic accounts can provide wonderful insight into Chinese environmental issues, particularly Jonathan Watt's well-researched and passionate *When a Billion Chinese Jump* (2010b). Also valuable are Colin Thubron's *Shadow of the Silk Road* (2007) and his earlier *Behind the Wall: A Journey through China* (1989), Paul Theroux's book of Chinese train travel, *Riding the Iron Rooster* (1988), and George Schaller's memoir, *The Last Panda* (1993), which provides a wonderful account of WWF's encounters with the Chinese bureaucracy as the first Western environmental NGO in China. Peter Mattheissen's 1978 classic, *The Snow Leopard*, conveys the fragility, mystery, and beauty of the Tibetan Plateau, while Mark Hertsgaard's travelogue, *Earth Odyssey* (1998), has some excellent chapters on China. Wonderful documentary films about China's environmental challenges such as "Warriors of Qiugang" and "Waking the Green Tiger" are now available; we mention some of the best of these at the ends of the chapters and hope you will use them to see both how polluted and how beautiful China can be, and to "meet" some of the public figures, activists, and ordinary people who play roles in this book. Recommended scholarly works can be found in the reference list.

OVERVIEW

The themes and analytical concepts of globalization, governance, national identity, civil society, and environmental justice will recur in the following chapters. The next chapter, which deepens our understanding of how globalization affects China's environmental challenges, presents broad trends, as well as drivers of China's environmental challenges such as population increase, the rise of the middle class, globalization and industrialization, urbanization and loss of arable land, and climate change. Chapter Three introduces the institutional and legal framework of China's governance system, which remains largely top-down even as limited decentralization has unleashed the market and empowered regional and local leaders. Chapter Four provides the historical and cultural context for China's changing national identity and the way decisions affecting sustainability are shaped by that context. Chapter Five investigates the changing possibilities for public participation in environmental governance, as well as civil society efforts to exert influence from the bottom up. Finally, Chapter Six investigates displacement of environmental harm across time and space, making the argument that China and the world are shifting the burden to future generations, to vulnerable populations in less powerful nations, within China proper to "peripheral" border areas primarily inhabited by ethnic minorities and the poor, to rural farmers, and to marginal urban populations. The Conclusion argues that China and the planet are at a pivotal moment in which the choice for more sustainable development models is still available, but that making this choice will require humility, creativity, and rejection of business as usual. The window will not be open much longer. Failure to act in a timely fashion to slow the ongoing transformation of the planet may result in unspeakable harm to natural systems, biodiversity, and landscapes, and may destroy many of the ineffable qualities that make human life so precious, not only in China but elsewhere in the world. In this, the world's people have a common interest.

Like any author, I hope that this book will find a wide audience, not only in the West but also in China. While it is written primarily for students of global environmental politics and contemporary China, it is also intended for any thoughtful person who seeks a better understanding of some of the core issues of our time. I hope that this introduction to China's environmental challenges will spark debate, create appreciation for the complexity and difficulty of the choices that China faces, and promote the understanding that what happens on the other side of the world is ultimately also happening in one's own back yard. It does not pretend to be a complete account of the dynamics of environmental change in such a huge country; the pace of change is too rapid and local conditions are too varied. For this reason, every chapter ends not only with a list of questions for discussion but also with a list of additional resources, most of them accessible electronically. I hope that this book will empower readers to engage with these problems, to participate in the global effort to identify their solutions, and to understand that the decisions they make as citizens and consumers truly matter. The "butterfly effect" articulated by chaos theorist Edward Lorenz, which describes how a butterfly flapping its wings can eventually create a hurricane through a series of cascading events, is more relevant than ever in today's tightly interconnected world.

QUESTIONS FOR RESEARCH AND DISCUSSION

1 Do people in developing countries such as China have an inherent "right" to the same living standards as those in the developed world? If so, what mechanisms should be in place so that such equity can be achieved?

2 Can China develop first and clean up later, as much of the developed world did, or is this no longer an option given the limits of the planet's resources? Can the international community reasonably expect the global South to follow a different path than that of the developed North? Does the developed world's standard of living have to change if we are to keep from planetary ecological collapse?

3 Can you apply the concepts of globalization, national identity, and environmental justice/displacement of harm to your own country? How do they affect your country's environmental footprint?

4 Discuss the civil society groups of which you are a member or which are active in your community. Does the state play a role in these groups? Do these groups shape state or local policies? Do they shape your attitudes and behavior? How might the situation be different in China?

ADDITIONAL RESOURCES

- "China Dialogue." An online publication and blog about Chinese environmental issues in English and Chinese, available at www. chinadialogue.net.
- China Environment Forum, Woodrow Wilson Center for International Scholars in Washington, DC. Reports, publications, and lectures available on line.

- *China Rights Forum*, "China at a Crossroads," available at: http://www.hrichina.org/crf/article/5423
- Ecological footprint information and quizzes: http://www.footprintnetwork.org and http://www.myfootprint.org
- Joseph Kahn and Jim Yardley, "Choking on Growth." Series and discussion available on the *New York Times* website.

2	Environmental Challenges: _____
	Drivers and Trends

The study of sustainability, whether long-term or short-term, local or global, inevitably engages questions of security, conflict, and threats to basic human welfare. Along with traditional security considerations such as military conflict over territory, scholars, policy makers, and development institutions are starting to understand threats to human well-being as coming from non-traditional sources such as environmental change, which may contribute to a sense of insecurity as people feel less confident of their livelihoods or that their basic needs will be met. Environmental scarcity can create tension and dislocation, while "abundance" can also, ironically, create rivalry and spur conflict as powerful forces to try to gain control over valuable resources. Environmental change tends to initiate additional shifts in the form of feedback loops, as people respond to challenges with practices that often further degrade the land. As part of the effort to analyze and predict both international and domestic instability and to identify the conditions for a secure and meaningful human life, major political institutions and development agencies have put great effort into identifying key trends and drivers of change. Major institutions that regularly issue relevant reports on China, and on Asia more broadly, include the World Bank (see, e.g., Dasgupta 1997; Johnson et al. 1997; Crooks 2001), the Asian Development Bank, the U.N. Economic and Social Commission for Asia and the Pacific, and the Japan Environmental Council, as well as civil society groups with serious research agendas such as Forest Trends and the World Resources Institute. Government institutions such as the U.S. Department of State and the Congressional-Executive Commission on China also issue important annual reports that are well worth consulting.

For our purposes, salient current drivers of environmental change in China are similar to and yet different from the main drivers of change throughout the world. They include: population increase, the rise of the Chinese middle class and concomitant changes in their consumption patterns, globalization of trade and manufacturing, changes in land use and loss of arable land due to urbanization and development, and climate change, which induces glacier melt, sea-level rise, violent weather, and droughts and floods, and is both an effect of environmental change and a driver of additional environmental transformation. These underlying forces and trends that push transformation are often not immediately visible; they operate at a level that can seem removed from the events of day-to-day life. However, by identifying these drivers we can often project where societies are heading and understand more clearly why some problems are so very difficult to resolve. (Less quantifiable drivers of environmental change include the state itself, with government-driven development plans and policies, and China's complex historical legacy of nature conquest and political upheaval; these will be addressed elsewhere.) This chapter also provides an overview of key recent environmental events and incidents, beginning with the Songhua River benzene spill of 2005. It concludes with general trends in policy making, intellectual life, and public participation.

POPULATION INCREASE

Since the Communist Party took power in 1949, the Chinese population has more than doubled, expanding from about 600 million to 1.3 billion (World Bank 2011); it is projected to reach nearly 1.5 billion by 2030. A Mao-era saying, "Every mouth has two hands," helps explain why the government was slow to realize the negative implications of the exploding population for meeting development needs. Mao came to power as a soldier who appreciated the value of a large army, while China's Soviet "elder brother" the U.S.S.R., which dominated the post-1949 policy environment, had lost so many troops during World War II that it was rewarding women who had large families as "mother heroes." Ma Yinchu, the demographer who tried to warn Mao about the dangers of large families, was silenced during the 1957 Anti-rightist Movement. By the time the draconian one-child family policy was introduced in 1978, it was too late to stabilize the population at a size that would not strain the country's resource base (Shapiro 2001). Nowadays, despite the sheer crush of the country's numbers, which are evident to anyone who has walked the streets of China's major cities, the government is more permissive about family size. This is because of the effectiveness of the last three decades' population control policies and growing concern about an aging population with few dependants to care for its seniors. Rural couples whose first child is a girl, ethnic minorities, and people without siblings are generally permitted second children as long as they are spaced apart, and in March 2011 the government signaled that it would permit additional relaxations, especially since urban couples seem uninterested in having many children because of the expense. In any event, China's enormous population size has made providing basic livelihoods for so many people, with such limited arable land, an enormous ongoing challenge.

For some Chinese analysts such as Qu Geping, the elder statesman of Chinese environmentalism and the author (with Li Jinchang) of a book called *Population and the Environment in China* (1994), almost all of China's environmental problems can be traced to overpopulation, whether land availability, degradation of forests and grasslands, or scarcity of water, minerals, and energy. Qu takes a practical, if utilitarian, view of conserving such "resources" as grasslands, forests, and minerals through improved population control, efficiency, and education. Qu, who attended the 1972 United Nations Conference on the Human Environment in Stockholm, was China's highest ranking environmental official for many years as Chairman of the Committee on Environmental and Natural Resource Conservation in the National People's Congress; he also served as top official in the State Environmental Protection Administration (later Ministry of Environmental Protection). The focus on the connection between overpopulation and environmental degradation is widespread among Chinese; indeed, if you ask about China's environmental problems, almost all mention what they call Mao's greatest mistake, his belief that "In many people strength is great" [*ren duo liliang da* 人多力量大].

The emphasis on human overpopulation as a root cause of environmental degradation is shared by many Western environmentalists, including Paul Ehrlich and John Holdren (1971), who are credited with creating an equation that describes environmental impact as a function of population, affluence, and technology (commonly written as the equation $I = PAT$). It seems obvious on the face of it that a growing human population exacerbates pressure on land and resources, increases pollution, and may even surpass the "carrying capacity" of a geographic region or even the planet, leading to ecosystem collapse. Moreover, affluence seems obviously to bring greater consumption of goods, with all of their impacts on the earth. Technologies such as toxic chemicals and machines that allow us to extract resources are modern inventions which evidently contribute to the problem even as they seem to bring us higher standards of living and at times offer hope for environmental clean-up. That said, finding the root causes of environmental problems is not so easy, for problems tend to be interconnected via positive and negative feedback loops. What is the root cause of overpopulation? Should we also be looking at government and family failure to educate little girls? Indeed, development professionals know that, statistically speaking, the better educated the woman, the smaller her family size. Should we look at social factors such as the lack of public assistance for retirees in the countryside, which make families feel as if they need many children, or at traditions of exogamy, in which the female joins her husband's family after marriage, which lead to a preference for boys? Should we also look at the fact that in developing countries traditional families' power often rests on the size of their clan? Today, you will find many Chinese towns and villages that take their names from a single family, in an echo of the ongoing influence of that ancient political structure.

China's fertility rate is now low in global terms, and population is expected to stabilize in a decade or two and to decrease slightly thereafter, a statistic of little consolation in a world set to reach a population of more than nine billion by 2050. Although urban Chinese are generally accepting of the one-child family policy and gender equality is well established in the cities, China's farmers, understandably worried about having enough hands to work the fields and sons to look after them in their old age, still favor boys. This may be changing, however: Increased urbanization in the countryside, or, as the Chinese slogan has it, "leave the land but don't leave the region" [*litu bu lixiang* 离土不离乡], may continue to lower birth rates overall, and so many rural Chinese are now migrating to large cities that conventional generalizations about rural versus urban birth rates may soon no longer apply.

RISE OF THE MIDDLE CLASS

Sheer numbers of people may not be as important as their consumption and production capabilities. Another driver of environmental change and degradation is thus the global culture of affluence and consumption, a lifestyle and value system which has now been adopted in China. The growing middle class now aspires to own automobiles, live in spacious homes and apartments with comfortable and fashionable furnishings, eat higher up the food chain by switching from grain to meat-centered diets, and increase household energy use by using more appliances, heat, and air conditioning. Consumption patterns encourage resource extraction and production of luxury goods. For example, in 2010, the Chinese automobile market was the largest in the world with 17.2 million light cars and commercial vehicles sold domestically, far surpassing the runner-up United States with 11.6 million sold (J.D. Power and Associates 2011).

The same year, China's luxury goods market for sales of expensive brand name products such as watches, handbags, shoes, jewelry, and clothes totaled more than $10 billion, and is projected to hit $27 billion by 2015, or some 20 percent of the world market (Atsmon et al. 2011). The Chinese desire for the globalized Western lifestyle, modeled in films and observed through travel, is amplified by cultural traditions and recent history, which place a premium on conspicuous consumption, status symbols, and lavish gift-giving. The Chinese have suffered more than a century of privation and pent-up desire for material goods, and the newly affluent are enjoying their buying power to the utmost.

However, such consumption is fraught with risks and the low quality of Chinese products has become a shared global concern. All too often, "Made in China" means "Danger: Buyer Beware," as revealed during recent scandals over product quality of Chinese exports. Chinese cough syrup has killed children in Panama while pesticide-contaminated Chinese spinach was banned in Japan. Fish can be full of antibiotics and heavy metals. Tire treads separate, tainted pet food has caused renal failure in companion animals, toddlers' toys imported from China have been coated with lead paint, tooth-paste sweetened with antifreeze. At home, Chinese consumers have lost confidence in the safety of their food, while confidence in air and water quality is lower still. This is reflected in the widespread purchase of bottled drinking water which has itself often been drawn from the tap by unscrupulous sellers, and in the willingness to pay a premium for imported and "green" food products. Several years ago, China was already second in the world in hectares of land under organic management (Paull 2007). However, a survey recently concluded that 70 percent of Chinese still fear for the safety of their food (MacLeod 2011), and in September 2011, state news agency *Xinhua* reported that 80 percent of Chinese doubt the safety of their beverages, citing illegal additives and toxic substances as their main concerns.

The newly affluent, in a better position to complain than the poor, are acutely aware of their dangerous and unhealthy living situations. Tainted food, unsafe consumer products, toxic air and water, and hazardous highways and public transportation systems mean that skyrocketing economic growth has done less to raise living standards than it appears. Citizen outrage is quick to ignite when a local accident or scandal occurs, creating a volatile and threatening situation for a government which struggles to hold onto its legitimacy and keep the populace disciplined.

The central Chinese government's response to revelations about accidents and toxicity is often damage control, denial, and counter-accusations. However, after a 2008 milk powder contamination scandal, it moved to streamline its product safety and food inspection bureaucracy and to clarify regulations which prohibit the production of fraudulent and adulterated products. It strengthened institutions such as the State Food and Drug Administration (expanded from the State Drug Administration) and conducted sweeping shutdowns of thousands of small food producers, in part for industrial restructuring but also to improve inspection capacity. Similarly, after the crash of a new bullet train in July 2011, when there was a public outcry over the government's efforts to force the media to report heart-warming stories about a rescued infant rather than about the people who were killed, the state announced a temporary halt to new high-speed train projects. Chinese courts have in recent years sentenced to death more than a few agency heads, mayors, and factory leaders charged with responsibility for industrial accidents and flagrant safety violations. However, such sentences and crackdowns speak to the government's need to be perceived as taking action rather than to the prospect that an airtight system of inspection and enforcement will soon be in place.

These efforts are top-down measures that fail to empower Chinese consumers to act upon their indignation. If China is to correct its dangerous consumer product and public safety situation, there must be improved access to information through honest labeling as well as a legal system capable of redressing harm and enabling Chinese citizens to gain oversight over public health and safety (challenges, admittedly, for developed countries as well). To date, Chinese consumers and victims of public health hazards have few avenues for redress other than taking to the streets and calling government complaint lines. Such actions occasionally meet with success but more often are suppressed or ignored. By Chinese law, consumers are entitled legally to recoup only double the price of a defective product. Moreover, the class-action lawsuit is underutilized and poorly understood as a consumer protection tool, and it is difficult to get courts to accept such cases.

Some environmentalists take heart in the rise of the middle class despite the increase in consumption and concomitant resource use. They cite the "environmental Kuznets curve," which posits a connection between income levels and environmental clean-up. According to this economic theory, which is popular among Chinese policy makers because it seems to justify taking more time to get pollution under control, pollution tends to be high at early stages of national development, but when basic needs for material goods are met, citizens start to focus on less tangible quality-of-life issues such as clean air and water. They also acquire the political clout to demand them, so an inverted U graph can be drawn to show that a rising middle class correlates to an improvement in indicators of environmental degradation (Stern 2003). Examples of the middle class's impatience can be found in Beijing, where, as Andrew Jacobs writes in the *New York Times* (2011), anger over polluted air spiked with the U.S. Embassy-Beijing's regular release of its rooftop air pollution monitoring data, which showed "hazardous" air on many days that the Chinese government's figures claimed its pollution is "moderate" or "slight." A Chinese micro-blogger's poll on whether the government should adopt stricter standards elicited tens of thousands of votes in favor of immediate adoption, leading the Beijing air pollution monitoring center to start offering limited public tours and the city's environmental bureau to promise that it would soon regulate the dangerous small particles released by vehicles. Whether such regulation would be effective is another matter entirely.

Unfortunately, the Kuznets curve model when applied to the Chinese environment rests on several shaky assumptions. It requires, first of all, that there be sufficient natural resources available to support the massive economic expansion required to generate a large enough middle class to apply sufficient pressure to reduce pollution and environmental destruction. It also assumes that environmental resources will be in a condition to be rehabilitated after development inflicts heavy damage. Finally, for the model to work the government must be in a strong enough position to respond positively to middle class demands, which is far from the case in today's China, where good environmental laws and regulation often go ignored. In fact, despite the best efforts of some government regulators and policy makers, new product and food safety scandals are in the news all the time. Finally, and most importantly, the planet cannot afford to wait for China to pass through the same stages of industrialization and clean-up followed in much of the developed world. The environmental Kuznets curve seems a pipe dream in the context of global patterns of environmental degradation, which indicate that the planet is at a tipping point with respect to many environmental indicators. Another model is required.

GLOBALIZATION OF MANUFACTURING

China's population numbers, and the people's growing affluence, may pale in significance as drivers of environmental change when one considers the globalized system of resource consumption and waste production to which they are connected. Much of the pollution that so troubles China's rising middle class is due to the fact that China has become a manufacturing powerhouse for the world: China's demand for resources is being driven not only by domestic consumers but also by international ones. We can more easily see the connection between China's problems and our own lifestyles if we consider the political economy of China's manufacture and export of consumer goods. The value of China's exports in 2008 was 146 times greater than in 1978 at the beginning of the economic reforms, an enormous increase that brings China to number two in the world. More than 94 percent of China's exports in recent years have been manufactured products such as electronics, toys, textiles, and furniture (WTO 2011). The huge scale of China's manufacturing apparatus is dramatically chronicled in the documentary film "Manufactured Landscapes," which chronicles in slow-moving detail the football field-sized sweatshops that power China's economic growth and the world's consumption.

One of the most useful tools for understanding global political economy is "commodity chain analysis," which traces a given raw material from its source to the consumer. We can look at China's import of raw materials such as minerals and timber from Southeast Asia and Africa and its export of finished products to developed countries, with nearly 40 percent going to the European Union and United States alone (WTO 2011), although an increasing percentage of such products are destined for the Chinese domestic consumer. This analysis demonstrates that end-users in developed countries are key participants in a linked chain that moves from poor nations to rich ones, depleting "natural capital" that cannot be replenished.

Consider the example of wood products. In 1998, China suffered devastating floods and the government banned logging on the headwaters of the Yangzi and other Western rivers to protect watersheds from erosion and improve flood control. Although not always thoroughly enforced, the ban shifted logging, much of it illegal, to places such as Cambodia, Myanmar, Indonesia, Eastern Russia, and as far afield as Gabon. A 2007 investigation by the *Washington Post* followed the trail of illegal logging in Myanmar and other parts of Southeast Asia all the way to such Western retailers as Home Depot and IKEA. The dynamic works like this. Logs are harvested in countries with weak environmental laws and/or corrupt governments; officials are bribed (or actually conduct the business) at every step of the way; false papers are issued as the timber changes hands to disguise its illegal origins; it crosses the border and brokers sell it to Chinese furniture factories that may or may not be aware of its origins. In this way, trees from the world's remaining tropical forests are converted into furniture, much of it exported to the West. In effect, China's growth depends on such imports of timber and other raw materials, so China's officials turn a blind eye. As the *Washington Post* put it, "The industry that connects forests in Asia with living rooms in the United States via the sawmills of China is a quintessential product of globalization" (Goodman and Finn 2007). According to researchers from the advocacy group Forest Trends, China's wood imports roughly tripled from 1997 (one year before the logging ban) to 2009. At the same time, the country's wood product exports have increased almost 700 percent in value (Sun and Canby 2010). When Western consumers make their purchases, few ask where the wood in their new patio set or designer flooring comes from, or are aware of the Forest Stewardship Council's efforts to certify and promote sustainably harvested wood, or consider the tremendous rate at which the planet's last remaining tropical and old growth forests are being lost. Such commodity chain analysis, which can also be done for other reprocessed resources such as minerals, can even be extended to uncover where such materials, including toxics, are discarded, thereby revealing the hidden costs of consumer buying power from a product's cradle to grave. Unfortunately, China's weak regulatory capacity is a problem for global "chain of custody" tracing efforts, since even well-meaning officials and factory managers have difficulty verifying the sources of their raw materials.

LAND USE CHANGES: URBANIZATION, INDUSTRIALIZATION, AND LOSS OF FARMLAND

China is poorly endowed with farmable land and its water resources are unevenly distributed both geographically and seasonally. It has nearly a quarter of the world's population but only five percent of its water resources and seven percent of its arable land (Brandon 2011). China's limited farmland was squeezed to maximum productivity through centuries-old traditions of terracing, fertilizing, and irrigation, and fared especially poorly during the "war on nature" of the Mao years, which saw attacks on sparrows, rainforests, and wetlands as part of an effort to secure grain (Shapiro 2001). Pressure on the land has become even more intense with rapid industrialization and real estate development. The government acknowledges that some of the changes in Chinese land use are unsustainable.

Like other Chinese statistics, figures on urbanization are unreliable, but some indicate that by 2030 a billion Chinese people, or 70 percent of the population, will live in cities. They will be concentrated in nearly 220 cities with populations of more than a million people, including, by 2025, eight megacities of more than 10 million inhabitants (Woetzel et al. 2009). Indeed, the Chinese Academy of Social Sciences' *Blue Book on China's Society* reported that by the end of 2011 for the first time more than one half of all Chinese people were urban residents (*China Daily* 2011b). New cities are being created in formerly rural areas to deal with unemployment and to try to stem migration to major cities, which the state views as a major challenge. Restrictions on residency rely upon the antiquated residence card system which once kept farmers in place by limiting their holders' access to ration coupons for food and rights to obtain housing, education, and health care; nowadays, with consumer goods so freely available on the open market, the residence card system has lost much of its power to restrain, and peasants often leave the countryside to join "floating populations" of temporary workers and housemaids in major urban centers. More than 200 million of these technically illegal residents live in makeshift slums with poor sanitation, limited access to medical care, and crowded living conditions (Bai 2008). Their children are not permitted to enroll in state schools, and the informal schools that have sprung up have often been abruptly dismantled, as authorities seek to drive migrants back home. In addition to economic incentives, another push toward urbanization is that local officials are often keen to sell arable land to real estate developers, as such sales are a prime source of income. Farmers are often driven off the land against their will, without adequate compensation for loss of land and livelihood.

With arable land per capita only 40 percent of the world average (Zhou 2002), China's government strives to protect remaining farmland. In August 2011, *Xinhua* reported government desires to safeguard 1.8 billion *mu* (296 million acres) of arable land to shore up grain security. But the fast pace of urbanization and industrialization combined with other land use changes have threatened even that minimum area. According to a report by U.N. special rapporteur Olivier De Schutter, "Since 1997, China has lost 8.2 million hectares (20.2 million acres) of arable land due to urbanization or industrialization, forest replanting programs, and damage caused by natural disasters. 'Today, 37 per cent of China's total territory suffers from land degradation. …This shrinking of arable land represents a major threat to the ability of China to maintain its current self-sufficiency in grain, and it fuels competition over land and land evictions'" (UNOHCHR 2010).

More stringent central government farmland preservation policies have slowed the rate of loss, but local development speculators and government officials' land grabs for construction and development have become a source of widespread social conflict and unrest. In one of the most dramatic recent examples, in December 2011 thousands of residents of the fishing village of Wukan in Guangdong province revolted openly against the government for such seizures, a standoff that lasted more than a week and resulted in the death of at least one villager.

CLIMATE CHANGE

Climate change is both an outcome of environmental change and a major cause of it, and it is the last driver that we will consider here, although it may be the most devastating and difficult to control. Climate change alters rainfall patterns and promotes sea level rise and strong storms, droughts and floods. These lead to cascading environmental effects such as desertification and erosion. Glacier melt in the Tibetan Plateau has an impact on the Yellow River and China's irrigation network in North China (Immerzeel et al. 2010). The aquifer below the North China Plain, fed by the increasingly parched Yellow River and the largest alluvial plain in East Asia, created through years of river-deposited sedimentation, is already falling by a meter per year and is set to be depleted within 30 years (Kahn and Yardley 2007). At the same time, aquifers which serve the huge city of Beijing continue to fall due to overuse for farming, industry, and household consumption. Extreme weather patterns have included violent storms and floods, while sustained droughts have been among the worst in centuries. Sea level rise could challenge the spectacular modernization of coastal cities like Tianjin and Shanghai, where there are already plans to build a water gate to combat flooding from increased storms. International scholars in 2007 published a detailed study suggesting that climate change could be devastating for China's large Eastern cities (Balk et al. 2007), as the country's densely populated coastal areas are among the world's most vulnerable to sea level rise and increased flooding from intense storms. Other organizations such as the

Intergovernmental Panel on Climate Change have made similar forecasts for coastal areas throughout the world.

Chinese experts warn that climate change will also affect China's grain harvest, reducing yields of rice, wheat, and corn, threatening food security, and leading China to import more staple foods (which then has an impact on global prices). In November 2011 the *China Daily* quoted Tang Huajun, a deputy dean of the Chinese Academy of Agricultural Sciences, as saying, "The impact of climate change, especially extreme weather and plant diseases and insects, will cause a bigger grain production fluctuation in China and bring more serious threats to the country's food supplies."

Climate change directly degrades the environment, but it also exacerbates a feedback loop of human-induced secondary degradation when humans fail to adapt in an intelligent way: drought causes a need for increased irrigation, which all too often causes salinization and lowered water tables, causing further land stress which then also leads to increased use of chemical fertilizers, which then leads to eutrophication, and so on. How China's government will approach the problem of "adaptation" (as distinct from "mitigation," which tries to address the causes rather than the effects), is a critical policy question for coming decades.

Almost all of China's major rivers flow from the glacier-rich Tibetan Plateau. When glaciers melt, rivers flood and then fail to replenish, and this threatens their basic ecological character and the life force that sustains China's population. China's per capita water resources are already among the lowest in the world, at just one-fourth of the world average (Xie 2009). Admittedly, there are mixed scientific findings as to the severity and timing of changes in glacier melt, and social, economic, and political as well as environmental drivers affect water scarcity in North China. However, policy makers are so worried that North China, including Beijing, could run out of water that they are building channels to transfer water from the Yangzi to the Yellow River, a megaproject with its own problems of human rights abuses, forcible relocations of up to 300,000 people, and pollution (Freeman 2011). Yet if something is not done, massive water shortages could turn the people of North China into "climate refugees," people who are displaced because of environmental transformation due to climate change.

Another consequence of climate change is severe weather patterns. In Inner Mongolia and neighboring Ningxia province, sustained drought combined with severe winter has killed millions of cattle and forced farmers and herdsmen to dig ever deeper wells. Nomads are being forced to settle in cities, with few urban skills. Meanwhile, in Central and Southern China, severe flooding after periods of drought has displaced entire towns and caused leaders to acknowledge that their confidence in the massive Three Gorges Dam's capacity to control and withstand severe flooding may have been overly optimistic. Such natural disasters appear ever more common and severe, as is consistent with scientific predictions concerning the impacts of climate change.

China's own contribution to climate change is growing quickly. A definitive study from the University of East Anglia entitled "A Carbonizing Dragon" shows that China has overtaken the United States as the largest carbon emitter, primarily because of investment in heavy industry, infrastructure, and energy production; urbanization is itself a significant cause of increased emissions, as city living is more energy intensive than rural life (Minx et al. 2011). Emissions have grown about 10 percent per year since 2000 (Auffhammer and Carson 2008). Moreover, the Netherlands Environmental Assessment Agency recently found that even on a per capita basis, Chinese emissions are on track to match or exceed those of the average American by 2017.

The Chinese government is making strong efforts to deal with these problems. The "Scientific Development Perspective" [*kexue fazhan guan* 科学发展观], to use the official language of China's current guiding ideology, incorporates sustainable development and social welfare into the national goal of building a "Harmonious Society" [*hexie shehui* 和谐社会]. Chinese policy makers are well aware of the consequences of climate change, even as they argue that China is not responsible for most of it, and China is an eager recipient of "Clean Development Mechanism" funds and projects that reward developed countries for investing in climate change mitigating projects in the developing world (Morton 2005). China's State Council in November 2011 issued a "White Paper on China's Policies and Actions for Addressing Climate Change," laying out a roadmap for cutting carbon emissions. The report featured plans to reduce energy intensity per unit of GDP, cap total carbon output, initiate a pilot project for a carbon trading market, and set requirements to increase the use of non-fossil fuel energy sources from 8.6 to 11.4 percent. But China's electricity and fuel challenges are great, and despite Chinese leadership in solar and wind manufacturing, there is heavy reliance on domestic coal supplies and intense international competition to secure foreign supplies of fossil fuels. In 2007, coal-fired plants produced roughly 80 percent of China's energy (U.S. Energy Information Administration 2010). China is thus expected to continue to emit huge quantities of carbon dioxide. China's energy policy is expected to continue to emphasize energy intensity and increasing percentages of renewables (which China defines as including the often controversial big hydropower dams and nuclear power plants), while the use of fossil fuels in absolute numbers continues to rise.

Such trends are not inevitable. A November 2011 conference of the China Council of International Cooperation on Environment and Development, a group of 200 world experts on environmental policy who offer suggestions to the Chinese government, recommended that the country spend 5.77 trillion *yuan*, or about $909 billion dollars, before 2015 to make transitions away from polluting and energy-intensive industries. This would cost the country almost a million jobs and more than 100 billion *yuan* in economic output but save 1.43

trillion *yuan* in energy expenses while creating more than 10 million jobs and expanding the economy by more than 8 trillion *yuan*. The report warned that "the blind pursuit of economic growth has now become a huge obstacle for China's green growth," and that even with such investments, by 2020 the country will still face grave air pollution, water shortages, ecological degradation, and mounting piles of hazardous wastes (Li, Jing 2011).

RECENT EVENTS AND ENVIRONMENTAL CONFLICTS

Such drivers of environmental change as population growth, the rise of the middle class, globalization of manufacturing, land use changes, and climate change are difficult for the average person to perceive because they tend to be gradual and their impacts indirect. If you were to ask a Chinese citizen about the environment, he or she would probably instead mention pernicious pollution levels that foul the air and water, recent industrial accidents, food safety scandals, disputes over factories, and contention over infrastructure projects. He or she might also focus on regional problems, such as the overuse, pollution, and salinization of the Pearl River, which threaten the water supply of Guangzhou and Macao, or on local problems such as the solid waste crisis now occurring in Beijing. A Chinese citizen might also mention specific endangered species that have been widely discussed in the media in recent years, including pandas, the Tibetan antelope, Yunnan golden monkeys, or the Yangzi River dolphin.

Here, then, are just a few of the most well-known events of recent years, all of which would be familiar to any educated Chinese person concerned about environmental problems, and at least some of which may reflect the deep drivers of change listed above.

In November 2005, an explosion at a government-owned petrochemical plant in Jilin City caused a major spill of benzene, a highly carcinogenic chemical, into the Songhua River. This failure to maintain industrial production safety standards became an international incident when the government, whether out of insecurity or fear, failed to disclose the accident in a timely fashion to the citizens of downriver Harbin city, whose water supply was eventually shut off, or to the government of downstream Russia and the affected citizens living along the Heilong River in the neighboring Russian Far East. ("Duty to Notify" is considered a principle of customary international environmental law.)

In April 2007, water quality "eco-warrior" Wu Lihong, a crusader against industrial pollution in Jiangsu Province's Lake Tai, which provides tap water to the city of Wuxi, was arrested as a troublemaker for giving interviews to foreign journalists. He was officially charged with blackmailing the factories he was trying to shut down. His repression underlines the political risks that environmentalists and activist lawyers often face in an age of intense industrialization and globalization. In May 2007, a blue-green algae outbreak in the lake caused a drinking water crisis in the city of Wuxi on Lake Tai, where bottled water prices rose to six times their normal price.

Also in May 2007, cell phone text message-organized citizen resistance to a proposed Taiwan-China joint venture paraxylene (PX) chemical plant in Xiamen succeeded after a public demonstration of more than 20,000 residents gained the attention of local Party officials and the National People's Congress. One million text messages were sent warning that the chemical would cause birth deformities and leukemia. The factory is still planned for a less well-organized community in Zhangzhou, illustrating the fact that middle-class resistance to pollution does not in itself result in environmental improvements.

In May 2008, a devastating earthquake in Sichuan Province's Wenchuan County killed about 70,000 people, many of them children whose schools collapsed due to shoddy construction. Some environmentalists and geologists believe that the weight of the water in the reservoir behind the Zipingpu dam on the Min River, located only a few kilometers from a major fault line, may have contributed to seismic instability in the region or even triggered the quake.

The 2008 Olympics, held just a few months afterwards in August, marked the culmination of a period of intense attention to air pollution in Beijing. There was so much doubt about air quality that some athletes remained in Japan until the last possible moment and emerged from airplanes wearing face masks, to the chagrin and ire of Chinese hosts. The Chinese government exerted extraordinary efforts to ensure a blue skies event, building new subway lines, closing factories, and banning cars. They even seeded the clouds to induce rainfall in the days before the event to help settle pollution and ensure that there would be good weather for the opening ceremonies. Patriotic Chinese saw the successful event as a coming-out party for their country's re-entry to high status on the world stage, but pollution levels quickly returned to prior high levels after the Olympics ended. Local urban air quality improved briefly when factories like the notorious Capital Iron and Steel Factory Company were moved to rural areas, but high levels of pollutants still occur regularly over much of the Beijing region, driven in part by a massive increase in automobile sales and traffic that regularly jams Beijing's freeway system.

That same year, there was increased global attention to e-waste villages in Guangdong Province, where many of the cast-offs of the global trade in electronic equipment are recycled. A 2008 report broadcast in the U.S. on CBS television's "Sixty Minutes" spurred China to pass new regulations on recycling electronic equipment and to try to crack down on the lucrative illegal trade, but loopholes and problems with enforcement continue.

The years 2008 and 2009 saw protests and violent crackdowns in ethnic minority regions. In Lhasa, Tibet, a March 2008 protest soon spread to Tibetan areas in Sichuan, Qinghai, and Gansu Provinces. In

July 2009 a violent riot occurred in the capital city of Urumqi in the Xinjiang Autonomous Region. These were only the latest incidents in a long history of Tibetan and Muslim resentment of Han Chinese rule. Recent tensions have been exacerbated by infrastructure projects that facilitate the state's resource extraction, by Han in-migration, and by social policies that promote tighter social control over nomads and dissenters, who are made scapegoats for grasslands degradation that has much to do with policies that opened up remote territories during the Mao era, drained wetlands, and restricted the mobility of nomads.

In July 2010, two oil pipelines offloading imported crude oil from a tanker to a storage facility in China's Northeast port city of Dalian exploded, causing China's worst ever oil spill. A heroic clean-up by citizen volunteers and the People's Liberation Army masked uncertainty about the causes and size of the enormous spill.

In April–June 2011, 5,000 metric tons of chromium-contaminated carcinogenic chemicals were dumped in Yunnan Province's Qiujing Prefecture near the Chachong reservoir, threatening the Pearl River, which is the source of drinking water for tens of millions of people, including Guangzhou (Canton). In August, after 77 cattle died, police detained the two drivers and other employees of the trucking company that had been contracted to carry the waste to Guizhou Province.

The above list of recent environment-connected incidents could run to many more pages, including well-known localized struggles over the locations of waste incineration plants and publicity over "cancer villages," as well as ongoing campaigns against dam-building on rivers in Western China, most famously on the Nu River in Yunnan Province, where local leaders find the temptation to harness one of China's last remaining wild rivers for energy all but irresistible. We will explore some of these struggles in more detail in later chapters.

These newsworthy incidents and events have been accompanied by tremendous intellectual ferment and discussion at top policy-making levels, in think tanks and environmental NGOs, on university campuses, and among interested and affected ordinary citizens. Such open debate would have been all but impossible even a few decades ago. The educated public is paying increased attention to the connection between pollution and public health; prominent groups such as Greenpeace and former journalist Ma Jun's Institute of Public and Environmental Affairs are creating pressure for greater information transparency on water and air pollution, and there are ongoing efforts to create feasible "green accounting" systems. The central government is trying to institutionalize ways to reward local officials for environmental protection rather than economic growth, albeit with uneven success. Scholars, policy makers and activists are creating cutting-edge initiatives to try to shift China toward a sustainable development model, particularly through innovations in energy technology and pricing. Climate change is gaining greater public attention, as the droughts in Northern China have an impact on food prices and are being explicitly linked to extreme weather and Himalayan glacier melt; moreover, as elsewhere in the world, the Chinese are starting to focus on the effects of climate change on protected areas. As we have seen in this overview of trends and drivers as well as specific recent events, China is undergoing radical economic, social, and environmental change, perhaps unprecedented in world history: To be Chinese today is to face incredible opportunities and challenges. The factors outlined above express themselves in China in particular ways, and how China responds to them rests on specific governance structures that have evolved over the course of China's unique history, as we shall see in the coming pages.

QUESTIONS FOR RESEARCH AND DISCUSSION

1 Identify an environmental problem in your hometown or in China and draw a flowchart that captures the root causes and repercussions of that problem. How might scholars from different

disciplines approach this problem? Which perspectives do you find most useful?

2 Examine the products in your home and note where they were manufactured. How many come from China? Do you know where the raw materials in these products come from?

3 View Annie Leonard's 20 minute video, "Story of Stuff" (http://www.storyofstuff.org/movies-all/story-of-stuff/). Is it an accurate representation of the role of consumption in the global political economy? Are there biases? Where does China fit in?

4 How might climate change affect the place where you live? What direct or indirect effects do you see? Are there connections to environmental practices in China?

ADDITIONAL RESOURCES

- Asian Development Bank, China reports, available at: http://beta.adb.org/countries/prc/main
- Carla Freeman, "Quenching the Dragon's Thirst" (a study of the South-North Water Transfer), pdf available at the Circle of Blue website.
- China Climate Change Info-Net, available at: http://www.ccchina.gov.cn/en
- Peter S. Goodman and Peter Finn, "Corruption Stains Timber Trade," *Washington Post*, Sunday April 1, 2007. Article available on the *Washington Post* website.
- "Manufactured Landscapes," a documentary by Jennifer Baichwal about photographer Edward Burtynsky. Excerpts available on YouTube.
- McKinsey Global Institute interactive website on China's urbanization and other trends: http://www.mckinsey.com/Insights/

MGI/Research/Urbanization/Preparing_for_urban_billion_in_China

- United Nations Economic and Social Commission for Asia and the Pacific: http://www.unescap.org
- World Bank reports on water scarcity in China. Available on the World Bank/China website.
- World Development Indicators, World Bank: http://data.world-bank.org/country/china

3 | State-led Environmentalism: The View from Above

China remains a top-down, centralized, authoritarian state; this is true even despite the enormous new personal and economic freedoms of the past quarter-century and the emergence of a vital middle class that is coming into their own both as consumers acquiring material goods and as citizens demanding government accountability. Civil initiatives remain sharply curtailed, NGO activities are circumscribed, and the administrative and legal systems that might help China to enforce its environmental laws, some of which are excellent, remain weak. Well-intentioned environmental initiatives are often implemented in heavy-handed fashion, with negative implications for social justice. For example, Chinese citizens are being forcibly relocated in the name of such projects as the South-North Water Transfer Project, which is intended to carry water from the flood-prone Yangzi to the parched Yellow River from which North China gets its drinking water; minorities are subjected to "ecological migration," resettled from the grasslands of Inner Mongolia, Qinghai, Gansu and other parts of Greater Tibet in an effort to reduce the impact of herding; and the Three Gorges Dam has caused at least 1.2 million people to leave their homes, sometimes against their will and without the subsidies they have been promised, with more relocations to come because of unexpected problems with erosion. Millions more people across China are slated to be moved for initiatives to provide water, energy, and ecosystem restoration. Restrictions on public participation, debate, and access to information have meant that the science used to develop policies for sustainable development does not always reflect local conditions or human impacts and even contributes to official abuses of power.

Nevertheless, the Chinese central government deserves tremendous credit for trying to integrate environmental concerns into its plans, laws, and policies. One of the most significant trends in the past few decades is the growing importance of sustainable development in national planning documents and central-level statements and commitments. The Chinese state has moved away from its Mao-era isolation and public self-presentation as a developing country that needs the world's assistance and has become a constructive participant in the global dialogue on how to resolve major transnational challenges. Environmental issues have climbed toward the top of the domestic agenda of China's leading officials in response to growing public clamor about the impacts of pollution on health and quality of life. Policy makers at the highest levels of government have affirmed China's commitments to deal with the country's responsibility to mitigate global climate change, to improve energy efficiency, to carry out wide-scale conservation projects and stem desertification, and to tackle the intransigent problems of water and air pollution. Although there is an enormous implementation gap, these expressions of intention and commitment from the highest leadership are remarkable, as are independent efforts by the mayors of cities like Dalian and Tianjin. In a typically outspoken comment, high-ranking environmental official Pan Yue told the *Financial Times* in 2004, "If we continue on this path of traditional industrial civilization, there is no chance that we will have sustainable development. China's population, resources, environment have already reached the limits of their capacity to cope. Sustainable development and new sources of energy are the only roads we can take."

This chapter outlines what the Chinese government has done to date to try to achieve sustainable development. It discusses how that narrative fits into the Chinese desire to regain stature on the international stage by participating in negotiations and treaties and perhaps even pioneering a new development model that "leapfrogs" some of the mistakes of Western countries (Pan et al. 2011). While the desire to regain national greatness might seem to compete with the effort to achieve sustainable development, there is another, perhaps more encouraging way of looking at the Chinese government's choices: China can follow the Western version of industrial modernization, which has often involved unjust, ecologically destructive economic development, or the country can create a post-industrial idea of progress that embraces the tenets of sustainability. This debate is complex and involves a range of individuals, bureaucratic institutions, and locations.

GOVERNMENT STRUCTURE

There is fragmentation, both horizontal and vertical, in China's governmental structure. Competing and overlapping bureaucracies plague every level of administration, and the lines of authority from the "center" in Beijing to the localities are often weak, with environmental officials at the prefecture, district, county, and township levels often answering to other local officials rather than to their superiors in the central environmental bureaucracy. As a result there are competing perspectives on development and environment within the state, and differences of opinion as to how much attention to pay to the environment. Within the bureaucratic system there are strong advocates for a new, more ecological form of modernization, but they face serious challenges. The desire for sustainability competes with a "pollute first, mitigate later" [*xianwuran houzhili* 先污染后治理] ethos found in many branches of the government as well as among regional and local leaders who claim they are merely following the same pattern of development as modern industrialized nations and are too poor to prioritize environmental considerations.

To stimulate economic development and address poverty and potential unrest, China's leaders have in recent decades embarked on a program of decentralization, ceding many political and economic functions to the provincial and local levels. This has liberated economic actors, unleashing economic growth and entrepreneurial energy. However, such moves have made environmental policy implementation more difficult. The government is now attempting to continue strong centralized environmental policy making while improving on its weak implementation capacity at a time when local provinces, cities, and even towns enjoy great economic and political autonomy. A Chinese saying goes, "the heavens are high and the emperor is far away" [*tiangao huangdiyuan* 天高皇帝远].

In private conversations and even in official documents and news articles, central-level environmental officials often reveal frustration with provincial and local cadres. They complain that as soon as their backs are turned, local officials return to their polluting ways, or reopen those illegal coal mines that are so dangerous, or resume timber-cutting despite the logging ban. In 2006, the *South China Morning Post* quoted Zhou Shengxian, director of the Ministry of Environmental Protection (then the State Environmental Protection Administration), as blaming "the blind pursuit of economic development among local cadres over environmental protection" for problems with 21,000 chemical plants, 50 percent of them expelling effluent into the Yellow and Yangzi rivers and built without undergoing environmental impact assessments. Indeed, entrenched and corrupt power elites in remote areas sometimes act as if they hold sway over private fiefdoms, as confirmed in my own observations during a 2009 visit to Songpan, a town in Sichuan Province where local officials had appropriated for their own purposes a jeep purchased by a European environmental NGO within weeks of its arrival. A pair of local Chinese women I befriended on a hike in the hills told me that the same clan had controlled the town since the Cultural Revolution, and that wounds from that period remained raw.

Understanding the institutional, legal, and bureaucratic framework in which China's environmental policy making and implementation take place requires an introduction to the structure of the Ministry of Environmental Protection (MEP), regional and local Environmental Protection Bureaus and Offices, and the environmental legal framework. It also requires an overview of China's participation in international treaties and meetings in greater detail than that provided in prior chapters and a deeper appreciation of the challenges of implementation and enforcement.

The Communist Party of China is the unitary governing party (despite the nominal existence of a "united front" of other parties), with the General Secretary the most important national leader (former hydro-engineer Hu Jintao, expected to be succeeded by Xi Jinping) and a Politburo of 24 members, among which the Standing Committee of 9 members (the number varies) is most powerful. Trying to penetrate the opaque process of coalition building and jockeying by which leaders emerge is a major preoccupation of foreign China-watchers. Alongside the Party, and still largely controlled by it, are State government institutions, with the nearly 3,000 member National People's Congress (NPC) as the legislative body that approves laws and the general direction of the country through five-year plans negotiated in advance. Although the NPC has traditionally been a rubber-stamping body for the Party, it has in recent years shown more independence, as in 1992 when about one-third of the members refused to approve the Three Gorges Dam. The NPC elects a largely ceremonial Premier, currently Wen Jiabao, who was originally trained as a geologist.

The State Council of the People's Republic of China is the chief administrative authority in the country, chaired by the Premier. The 27 ministries and commissions under the State Council include several with overlapping jurisdiction over environmental matters, including the Ministry of Environmental Protection (MEP), Ministry of Water Resources, Ministry of Agriculture, Ministry of Housing and Urban-Rural Development (formerly Ministry of Construction), Ministry of Science and Technology, and Ministry of Land and Resources. At an administrative rank below the ministry level sits the State Forestry Administration. As an example of jurisdictional overlap, national and provincial parks may be established by the MEP, Ministry of Land and Resources, Ministry of Housing and Urban-Rural Development, or State Forestry Administration. The Ministry of Foreign Affairs has responsibility for negotiating China's international role in environmental treaties and obligations in accordance with positions decided by the Party.

China has signed or ratified many international environmental treaties, including the 1971 Ramsar Convention on Wetlands, the 1973 Convention on International Trade in Endangered Species (CITES), the 1987 Montreal Protocol on Substances That Deplete the Ozone Layer, the 1989 Basel Convention on the Control of Transboundary Movements of Hazardous Wastes and their Disposal, the 1992 United Nations Framework Convention on Climate Change (UNFCCC), and the 1997 Kyoto Protocol to the UNFCCC. Chinese officials have attended the key U.N. conferences, including the pivotal global environmental conferences in 1972 in Stockholm, 1992 in Rio, 2002 in Johannesburg, and 2012 again in Rio. Although, as a member of the negotiating block known as "China and the G-77," China has often helped to articulate developing countries' desires not to have to pay the price of developed countries' industrial revolutions and high rates of consumption, it has also since 1994 had an administrative center for China's Agenda 21 (the sustainable development action plan that emerged in 1992). Despite the fact that Agenda 21 is generally understood to be a weak institution, China gives it more attention than many developed countries. Moreover, the country has done a great deal to reduce the percentage of non-renewable fossil fuel resources in its energy mix. This is remarkable since China for many years had a reputation for being a spoiler in the climate change negotiations; government negotiators have insisted that as a developing country China has no obligation to undertake firm commitments to reduce its carbon dioxide emissions; it was not responsible for creating the crisis and has an unshakable right to development. Nevertheless, in 2007 the government passed a Medium- and Long-term Development Plan for Renewable Energy in China, which requires that 15 percent of China's energy come from renewables by 2020. China has also pledged to reduce CO_2 emissions intensity by 40 percent from 2005 levels, also by 2020. It appears that, in practice, China has accepted the principle of "common but differentiated responsibilities," a core tenet of international environmental law that acknowledges that all countries have a shared interest in dealing with our environmental crises.

China's Five-year Plans have also increasingly incorporated sustainable development goals, particularly the 12th Five-year Plan issued in spring 2011, which some journalists and policy makers have called the greenest in Chinese history. Many of the objectives to be achieved by 2015 are related to environmental issues and natural resources, including the intention of incorporating sustainability into Chinese manufacturing practices. During the prior Five-year Plan, from 2006 to 2010, China successfully reduced energy intensity by 20 percent, and the new target is to reduce it by an additional 16 percent. (Energy intensity measures an entity or country's efficiency of energy use per unit of GDP, as compared with absolute consumption; thus China's overall energy use is expected to continue to rise even as its energy intensity decreases, which is poor consolation for environmentalists who are concerned about the overall trajectory of energy use and climate change.) According to an analysis from *China Briefing* (Lam 2011), the goal is to raise non-fossil fuel use from 8 percent to 11.4 percent, cut CO_2 emissions by 17 percent and reduce several major pollutants such as nitrogen oxide (NO_X) and sulfur dioxide (SO_2).

The overall positive environmental impact of these efforts may be less than it appears, as the renewable mix includes hydropower and nuclear plants, which come with their own often severe environmental and social problems. Ecosystem disruption, forcible relocations, illegal approval processes and dangerous and shoddy construction plague China's dams, and battles over dams on the remaining free-flowing rivers in China are being fought in villages and in the courts, with opponents alleging inadequate environmental impact assessments, poor compensation plans for displaced people, and corruption by local officials who stand to benefit from dam construction. There is a vigorous and articulate anti-dam opposition movement both within China and in alliance with international groups. These are helping to focus attention on China's shift to building dams on the headwaters of international rivers, which may have significant negative impact on peaceful relations with neighboring states (Chellaney 2011). Nuclear energy has short-term and long-term risks of radiation leaks and explosions, plus immediate impacts on aquatic life near cooling systems. Considering China's terrible safety record in other industrial projects such as coal mines and factories, China and the world would do well to tread carefully. According to the World Nuclear Association, China had 14 nuclear power plants and more than 25 under construction as of November 2011. Although approvals for new plants were briefly frozen after the nuclear accident at the Fukushima plant in Japan in March 2011, more than 100 are planned by 2020. However, the energy picture is not entirely grim: There have also been impressive strides in the production of wind energy, particularly in Inner Mongolia (which has yet to be well integrated into the energy grid) and in solar energy, particularly in sun-drenched Tibet, where small-scale solar technology is widely adopted for greenhouses and cooking and larger solar plants are used in enterprises and industry. This protects vegetation while bringing energy into homes far from the conventional grid.

In a striking shift toward conservation, the number of national parks has steadily increased to more than 200, most of them falling under the jurisdiction of the Ministry of Housing and Urban-Rural Construction. Although a great many of these are "paper parks" that exist in official documents and regulations but not in practice, China is beginning to experiment with new management styles, in some cases charging high entrance fees and limiting access via park-run tour buses, as is done in many international parks. While this may be good for some of the species inside the parks, it can be bad news for local people who relied on providing horse rides and lodging to tourists, and it can increase rates of cultural disruption, as many of the people living near these parks are ethnic minorities. Such practices demonstrate awareness of the commercial value of ecotourism on the part of national and local leaders. In general, Chinese tourists tend to be interested in spectacular waterfalls or rock formations that resemble mythical creatures and provide good photo opportunities rather than in solitary hiking or wildlife viewing; getting a photo of oneself standing in front of a famous spot is often the main goal of such visits. Meanwhile, China's wildlife managers' approach to biodiversity tends not toward ecosystem preservation but toward wildlife farms and even cloning (as in the case of the Giant Panda) rather than preservation of habitat. Tellingly, Jonathan Watts (2010b, p. 289) cites tales of welcome banquets at nature reserves where the menu features endangered species.

Chinese environmental law dates to 1979 and the beginning of the post-Mao reform era, when the Environmental Protection Law of the People's Republic of China laid out responsibilities for pollution prevention and resource use. It established basic institutions, giving the Ministry of Construction (now Ministry of Housing and Urban-Rural Development) the environmental portfolio. It articulated "three magic weapons": environmental impact assessments, liability for polluters through pollution discharge fees, and the "three synchronizations" policy of implementing pollution control measures during the "design, construct, and operate" phases of a project (Sinkule and Ortolano 1995). The early environmental protection bureaucracy became the State Environmental Protection Administration (SEPA) in 1998, not becoming the cabinet-level Ministry of Environmental Protection (MEP) until 2008. It is still widely viewed as a weak institution compared with other long-established ministries with broad portfolios.

Environmental damage was criminalized in the mid-1990s through modifications to the legal code. Since then, many new environmental standards and regulations have been issued, providing a sophisticated and credible framework for achieving resource protection and pollution prevention. Indeed, China has a reputation for having some of the most thorough environmental laws in the world. Alex Wang of the Natural Resources Defense Council writes that since 1979,

China's environmental law framework has grown to include at least two dozen major statutes and countless State Council regulations, standards, and other legal-norm-creating documents. The major laws include the Law on the Prevention and Control of Atmospheric Pollution, Law on the Prevention and Control of Water Pollution, and the Environmental Impact Assessment Law. Laws now cover forestry, fisheries, wildlife protection, marine areas, desertification prevention, clean production, solid waste, energy, and numerous other areas. The amount of work put into developing a legal framework for environmental protection has been impressive (2006–2007).

During recent decades, Qu Geping initiated three significant reforms, first as director of the State Environmental Protection Administration, and later as chair of the Environmental Protection and Resources Conservation Committee of the National People's Congress (Marcuse 2011). In 1993, Qu persuaded many government departments to support a national media campaign to expose polluters and clean up the environment. Prior to this time, the media had avoided environmental issues for fear of appearing anti-socialist. Reporters then began to ferret out and publicize the names of polluters and their factories. According to Qu, the number of stories about the environment during the next 15 years totaled 220,000. The press called it a "green hurricane" cleaning up China. Tens of thousands of the worst factories were closed. However, pollution continued to build. In 1994, environmental groups were allowed to form, although they had to be registered under the authority of existing institutions. Qu's most important contribution, and the fulfillment of his lifelong ambition, was the passage of the Environmental Impact Assessment Law approved in 2003 and coming into effect in 2004. A key feature was a provision that allowed ordinary citizens to participate in the governmental assessment of major projects, like dams, that would have a significant environmental impact. The law, which requires developers to obtain approval from the Ministry of Environmental Protection before proceeding, has been difficult to enforce as some developers, including major power companies like Huaneng and Huadian Power, have often forged ahead without permits, willing to pay the relatively small fines from the MEP rather than wait for approval. However, the provision for public input has proved valuable to environmentalists, who use it to promote public debate and widen participation in environmental decisions, as discussed in a later chapter.

Overall, implementation of environmental protection laws remains weak. Indeed, legal scholar Charles McElwee (2011, p. vii) provides a long list of obstacles to implementation, including "low status of law as a means of achieving societal goals," "lack of capacity within the country's bureaucracies and legal institutions," "delegation of responsibility for environmental protection to local authorities," "strong influence of informal networks on the application and administration of laws and regulations," and "structural flaws in existing laws and regulations." The deeper problem, as noted above, is the culture of corruption and lack of confidence in the fair and equal application of law; every rule seems made to be broken. Legal provisions can be vague and enforcement statutes toothless; powerful officials and businessmen find ways around the regulations, and until recently very few polluters found themselves subject to criminal prosecution. This is the on-the-ground situation in which dams are built after minimal or no environmental impact review and illegal mines open, and then reopen after authorities shut them down. Real estate developers expropriate farmland and raze entire neighborhoods in the face of fierce resistance and deadly confrontations with residents as a development boom tramples the rights of families who have lived in their homes for generations; in 2010, the *New York Times* described how the Chinese have come up with a special term to describe the lonely "nail houses" of the last holdouts, whose houses stand alone when all others have been bulldozed away (Wines and Ansfield 2010). Many Chinese dream of the day that there will be "rule of law" rather than "rule by law," and justice will be handed down even to high officials and the "princelings" who are their children. I will never forget hearing a woman whose son had been arrested for a minor infraction ask her friends if anyone knew how to get a gift to the judge; when I lived in China in the post-Mao years, it was common for people to spend every penny beyond subsistence income on cigarettes, watches, and more expensive bribes for officials who controlled residence permits, housing, salaries, and passports. The same dynamic operates today and affects the state's ability to implement anti-pollution laws.

Some implementation challenges are structural: The Ministry of Environmental Protection has comparatively little enforcement power. It supervises Environmental Protection Bureaus (EPBs) and Offices in a pyramidal fashion opening downwards to the provinces, counties, townships, and so on (some localities did not even have EPBs until the 1990s). However, as political scientist Kenneth Lieberthal (2003) explains, the quasi-federal administrative system in China is a form of fragmented authoritarianism based on both verticality and horizontality. In China this is known as the *tiao-kuai* [条块], or "branches and lumps" arrangement. Functionally, as in the case of the environment, there is a vertical hierarchy, but territorially there is a competing horizontal level of authority held by provincial and local governments. In terms of rank, provincial governments hold status equal to central ministries. Therefore, in practice, a central ministry like the MEP cannot issue a binding order to a provincial government. Moreover, local governments are often funded by the same industries that the EPBs are supposed to regulate, leading to all kinds of perverse incentives. Environmental officials are often hired by and beholden to local Party and government leaders and answer to them rather than to their superiors in the environmental bureaucracy; indeed, local EPBs' budgets, leadership and personnel decisions, and decisions to close plants are still made by local governments (Economy 2004). Local officials have been given great power to implement central government goals of both economic growth and environmental protection; in cases where the goals conflict, they tend to favor growth and industrial activity. Because of their weak structural position, local EPBs must often obtain permission from the local government to close down enterprises, and EPB officials are beholden to mayors and Party chiefs and may even participate in the revenues from small-scale factories or mines either directly or through complex networks of relatives and friends. Local protectionism at the village level is rampant. While so-called Township and Village Enterprises (TVEs) have often been blamed for much of China's pollution, they have also been a lifeline out of grueling farm work for local peasants and provided towns and regions with important revenue (Jahiel 1997; 1998; Ma and Ortolano 2000).

Another complication for the MEP is that of bureaucratic overlap and contradiction in the central government apparatus. Other ministries such as the Ministry of Commerce have mandates to promote economic growth, while environmental issues such as the governance of rivers and lakes, including water use rights and pollution, are handled not only by the Ministry of Water Resources but also by regional river commissions as well as other ministries. Key environmental problems affecting farmland, such as erosion, salinization, heavy metals pollution, and desertification, fall primarily under the aegis of the Ministry of Agriculture. There are competing and conflicting emphases on growth, government legitimacy, clean development, and stability, creating a confusing policy-making landscape in which actors sometimes work at cross purposes or with uncertain lines of responsibility. Moreover, the emphasis on growth has filtered down into the entire Party-State apparatus, so that when they are evaluated for promotion, local officials tend to be rewarded for the economic activity they have spearheaded rather than for protecting the environment. Efforts are being made to change this calculus with rewards for environmental protection as well as growth, but success varies greatly from region to region and even from city to city. The result is that some cities, such as Xiamen and Dalian (ironically, the site of the oil spill mentioned in a previous chapter), have reputations as particularly "green," while coal-rich cities like Linfen and Taiyuan in Shanxi are famed for the intensity of their coal dust and air and water pollution.

Economic realities and concerns about unemployment and social unrest often push the government away from environmentally friendly action. The Ministry of Environmental Protection is hardly in a position to close the enormous state-run iron and steel plants in the great north-eastern rust belt, where unemployment is exceedingly high and shutdowns would mean even more job losses. To make matters more difficult, China is, in effect, sitting on a mountain of cheap coal, one of the dirtiest of fossil fuels. To expect China not to exploit this resource, or to exploit it only with the most up-to-date modern scrubbers and complex and expensive carbon capture and sequestration technologies (a method of re-introducing the carbon into the earth that is under discussion in developed countries) is unrealistic at best, and seems to be asking China to act in a manner more responsible than that of the developed world.

Despite the clear disincentive to move away from the heavy reliance on coal, several Chinese cities, including Beijing, are experimenting with pilot carbon trading schemes, a development that has been reported and is being watched around the world. Although it is party to both the U.N. Framework Convention on Climate Change and the Kyoto Protocol, as a developing country China has no obligation to set quantified carbon dioxide emission reduction targets and, like other countries, it has merely "associated itself" with the 2009 Copenhagen Accord to negotiate a post-Kyoto framework, without making firm commitments. Still, the country is doing much more on climate change than it is required to do under international law and during 2011 negotiations in Durban took a proactive and constructive position to pressure developed countries to do more. The Chinese seem to be looking for win-win solutions that both alleviate the particulate pollution that causes so much misery and poor health locally and, at the same time, go at least part of the way toward addressing the CO_2 emissions that are causing dangerous climate change in the global atmosphere. They have also poured money into greenbelt projects intended to hold the line on creeping desertification, the source of so many sandstorms, while also serving as carbon "sinks."

The government has partnered with industry to provide powerful incentives to develop renewable energy technologies, which now play significant roles in China's economy both domestically and in the export market (Mastny 2010). China is a major global competitor in markets like solar and wind energy. According to figures from the state-run *Xinhua* news agency, the country installed 16 GW of new wind power in 2010, 62 percent more than the year before, bringing total wind power capacity to 41.8 GW, the world's largest. While this is only a tiny fraction of the country's total energy mix, recent studies have shown that the potential for Chinese wind power is enormous. Wind power alone could supply all of China's power needs for the next 20 years if it were fully developed (Fairley 2009). As for solar, the 2011 bankruptcy and closure of such manufacturers in the United States put China well ahead of other countries in solar technology and export, with three-fifths of global production capacity. In the automotive sector, the government is investing billions of dollars in hybrid and electric vehicles with the intention of becoming the world leader in manufacturing greener cars. China is now the world's largest automobile market, surpassing the U.S. in 2011; unfortunately, despite government efforts, consumers seem less interested in "green" cars than in sport utility vehicles, according to a report in the *Guardian* by Jonathan Watts (2011). It will be important to see whether government and corporate persuasion can shift that perception and turn energy-efficient cars into status symbols.

Some Chinese scholars and policy makers have not been shy to confront the problems of achieving sustainable development; we have already noted high-ranking environmental leader Qu Geping's famous book on population and the environment in China. Among other top leaders, then-State Science and Technology Commission head Song Jian was proactive in mobilizing China's attention to environmental issues in advance of the 1992 Rio U.N. Conference on Environment and Development (UNCED). The most critical of the scholarly Chinese analyses is undoubtedly the influential 1998 book, *Grave Concerns: Problems of Sustainable Development in China* by two Chinese Academy of Social Sciences Environmental and Development Institute researchers, Zheng Yisheng and Qian Yihong (a link to a summary translation in English is at the end of this chapter). Their analysis sees the barriers to sustainable development as largely political, including poor coordination among bureaucratic agencies and between the center and local governments, as well as lack of implementation of environmental laws and regulations. Zheng and Qian argue that the collective property rights system under which land is not privately held, corruption, and failure to respect individual rights and laws are deep structural problems that will make it difficult for China to achieve its goals. While we may wish to debate their notion that privatization will solve China's environmental problems, we must admire their willingness to challenge such core principles of socialism. Even today, the Party holds to the fiction that land in private hands is being leased and ultimately belongs to the state, which creates many gray areas in the economy and a state of uncertainty about whether resources will be available to landholders in the future; those who favor privatization argue that certainty over land tenure would promote sustainable use for the long term.

Other measures to improve the country's environmental performance include a typically Chinese central government approach to social change: creating "model environmental cities." This is a throwback of sorts to the Maoist practice of finding model individuals or places that others are supposed to emulate. During the Cultural Revolution, agriculture was supposed to "learn from Dazhai," industry to "learn from Daqing," and model soldiers, workers, and peasants were glorified on postage stamps while ordinary citizens were made to "study" their lives. Many of these models were manufactured for propaganda purposes, which may explain why people nowadays tend to be skeptical of such campaigns. However, cities can benefit by competing for National Model City status, which they can then use to promote tourism, draw investment, and host international events, as the formerly dirty city of Shenyang did when attracting a horticultural exhibition; in 2006, 12 cities were labeled as national models for environmental protection but since then there have been numerous competitions and public ceremonies recognizing not only cities but also model industries and leading individuals. Of course, there is always a risk that in applying for model status a city will simply force polluting industries to relocate beyond the city limits, which is in effect what happened when Beijing cleaned up its air in preparation for the Olympics. Still, the effort to find a pattern that works and then replicate it in other cities may be a useful way to encourage wider adoption of best practices, as long as local conditions are also respected and the model is not imposed dogmatically. During the Mao period, a model was taken to an extreme when the labor-intensive hillside terraces of Dazhai were imposed throughout the country, with disastrous results for erosion in areas where slopes were too steep for the terraces or the terrain otherwise unsuited (Shapiro 2001).

The Chinese government's struggle to regulate its vast and complex society can be illustrated by the widespread incidence of lead poisoning from battery factories and smelters, the subject of a 2011 report by U.S.-based Human Rights Watch. Villagers in severely contaminated towns have faced stonewalling by local government officials, misinformation about testing and treatment, cover-ups, and government failure to shut down factories with egregious environmental violations. The *New York Times* told the story of one village in Zhejiang where large numbers of adults and children were found to have up to seven times the safe level of lead in their blood: A mob of 200 people rioted in the Zhejiang Haijun Battery Factory, smashing filing cabinets and windows in an outpouring of rage designed to get the government to pay attention (LaFraniere 2011).

The recent scandals around melamine additives in infant formula and milk powder, although they do not involve the environmental bureaucracy, illustrate the Chinese government's lack of power to supervise industrial practices. Melamine, a fertilizer additive, artificially boosts the nitrogen content of milk, thereby giving a false reading of higher protein content. Beginning in 2008, melamine was discovered as an illegal additive in milk powder and infant formula. In March of that year, an unusually high number of cases of infant kidney stones caught the attention of Nanjing Children's Hospital. From March to September, the incidence of kidney problems in infants surged. Doctors discovered that most had been fed formula produced by the Sanlu Group, a major dairy company based in Shijiazhuang in Hebei Province. Despite complaints from consumers and an increasing number of sick infants, and even after government authorities detected melamine in infant formula on July 24, Sanlu continued to sell melamine-contaminated milk powder until it was recalled on September 11. By December 2008 almost 300,000 infants had been made sick, among whom 51,900 were sent to hospitals and six died. In January 2009, the former chairwoman of the Sanlu Group was sentenced to life imprisonment; in November 2009 Geng Jinping and Zhang Yujun, two main producers and sellers of hundreds of tons of melamine-containing "albumin powder" which had been added to raw milk, were executed.

Amazingly, the national scandal and international loss of face over this problem, and the strong government response including removal and resignation of several governmental officials, an overhaul of the overly complex and overlapping food safety regulatory system, and increases in inspections, have not definitively resolved the problem. Twenty-six more metric tons of contaminated milk powder were confiscated as recently as April 2011. Understandably, then, Chinese parents are willing to pay high premiums to purchase products imported from the West for their children, while top government officials in Beijing get their food from contracted farms whose products are guaranteed to be safe. One of the most popular purchases by Chinese tourists traveling abroad is Western-produced vitamin supplements, which are believed to be safer and more effective than those manufactured at home. I have seen Chinese visitors spend hundreds of dollars on these.

The lead and melamine scandals show us clearly that governance involves far more than government – regulations, laws, and legal deterrents have not been adequate to prevent behavior where the profit motive is so much stronger than the risk of discovery, and where ethical standards have become so confused. Indeed, these examples are just two of many failures of the Chinese system to protect Chinese citizens. Accidents in construction, transport, mining, and industry are also common; factory fires and explosions are everyday events. As a Chinese blogger pled eloquently after a new high-speed train fell off a bridge in July 2011, "China, please stop your flying pace, wait for your people, wait for your soul, wait for your morality, wait for your conscience! Don't let the train run out off track, don't let the bridges collapse, don't let the roads become traps, don't let houses become ruins. Walk slowly, allowing every life to have freedom and dignity. No one should be left behind by our era." As reported in the *New York Times* (Johnson 2011), this blogger captures the fact that China's out-of-control development and growth pose dangers to the nation's very identity. Ecologists tell us that ecosystems can adapt if changes occur slowly, but when environmental tipping points are reached, cascading events can cause the whole system to collapse. With its pace of growth and lack of regulatory control, China seems to be flirting with these thresholds.

As we have seen in this chapter, the Chinese government cannot simply say the word and implement a law or policy. Governance, even in an authoritarian country, is a messy process and a policy or law on paper is not the same as achieving widespread compliance. This is especially true where state regulatory capacity is weak and non-compliance is widespread, and where the government weakens its own capacity through conflicting priorities such as maintaining economic growth and limiting unemployment and social unrest. Fortunately, other institutions, including citizens' groups, are now taking a role in influencing public behavior concerning the environment, exerting pressure despite the government's fear of what might happen if it made pollution and accident information more transparent. Before we turn to this rich topic, however, we need better to understand some of the historical and cultural factors that complicate China's efforts to achieve sustainable development. While we do not want to make too much of the role of national culture in diplomatic (or undiplomatic) behavior, and while not all scholars believe that political culture explains very much, in the next chapter we will explore the notion that there is a link between culture and the prospects for sustainability, not only in China but everywhere.

QUESTIONS FOR RESEARCH AND DISCUSSION

1 Given the overlapping and competing mandates of Chinese government bureaucracies, what needs to change to support better environmental governance? What are the differences among law, policy, regulation, implementation, and enforcement? How can we explain the disconnections among them in the Chinese case?

2 What would sustainable development in China look like? How should we understand the interactions among the many factors that contribute to environmental degradation? Are some factors more fundamental or difficult to deal with than others?

3 What might be some of the Chinese government's motivations in stressing sustainable development and environmental protection? Do you think the government is recognizing intangible values of sustainability such as health, well-being, and justice? Should the government merely reflect the values of the citizenry, or does the government have a responsibility to lead the Chinese people toward sustainable behavior?

4 What should China's role in international environmental politics be? How do the country's policy makers see their responsibilities under environmental treaties such as that dealing with climate change? Is China's position on climate change fair or obstructionist?

ADDITIONAL RESOURCES

- Charlie McElwee's environmental law blog, at: http://www. chinaenvironmentallaw.com
- *China Daily*, "Green China" blog, available at: http://www. chinadaily.com.cn/bizchina/greenchina/index.html
- U.S. Environmental Protection Agency's China Environmental Law Initiative, at: http://www.epa.gov/ogc/china/initiative_home.htm
- Congressional-Executive Commission on China, at www.cecc.gov
- Ministry of Environmental Protection (MEP) official English-language website, at: http://english.mep.gov.cn/
- U.S.-China Partnership for Environmental Law, at: http://www. vermontlaw.edu/academics/environmental_law_center/institutes_ and_initiatives/us-china_partnership_for_environmental_law/ overview.htm
- United Nations in China publications, at: http://www.un.org.cn/ cms/p/resources/5/index.html
- Zheng Yisheng and Qian Yihong (1998) "China's Environment, Politics and the Economy: Grave Concerns." Link to U.S. Embassy-Beijing summary translation: http://gaodawei.wordpress.com/ 2011/04/09

4 | Sustainable Development and National Identity _____

What are the cultural and historical contexts in which China is trying to achieve sustainable development, and how do they affect the prospects for success? We saw in the last chapter that, at least in its rhetoric, China's stated public commitment to sustainable development is strong. Implementation shortfalls notwithstanding, the government has integrated sustainability into its five-year plans, passed laws mandating an ambitious national renewable energy portfolio, invested in research and development for green technologies and clean air and water initiatives, and participated actively in international discussions of global environmental challenges. However, China's prospects for achieving sustainable development are clouded by a political system that restricts public participation in environmental decision making, a political culture of insecurity, and uncertainty over national identity at a time of enormous economic growth and social change.

National identity can be understood as encompassing core values, world views and self-understood history; it includes interpretations of where a given people stand at the present moment, as well as future dreams, goals, and ambitions for the destiny of the nation. National identity is socially constructed and malleable (Anderson 1983); it is contested by different social groups and manipulated by the state. The state controls the official version of history; in China, for example, the birth and triumph of the Chinese Communist Party are celebrated, but the excesses and ideological extremism of the Cultural Revolution are absent from textbooks, while public debate about its causes is stifled.

The state decides which holidays to celebrate: China marks political holidays such as October 1st, National Day; after Mao Zedong's death the Party relaxed restrictions on traditional festivals such as the Dragon Boat Festival that marks the drowning of the poet Chu Yuan and the Qingming day of reverence for ancestors, and thereby signaled that it was distancing itself from the Mao-era characterization of all traditional culture as feudal. The state decides what symbols to use on currency, as when it sent a strong message reasserting the legacy of Mao by putting his face on the reissued 100 *yuan* and other notes in 1999. As the great anthropologist Clifford Geertz (1973) has taught, national identity is bound up in values and world views that are captured through public symbols and rituals and which give citizens a sense of their connection to their communities and the meaning of their lives. These are all things that the state attempts to control, with varied success; many Han Chinese are skeptical about the official version of history, and non-Han minorities even more so.

Most of China's 55 recognized non-Han minority ethnic groups (comprising about one-tenth of the population) have different narratives, values, and traditions, despite the fact that the official version of Chinese history touts the integrity of Chinese geo-political borders and the long, unbroken history of the Chinese people. In fact, China's state-building process has been far messier and more complex than this. Territorial borders have shifted dramatically since the time of the "unifying emperor" Qinshi Huangdi (259–210 BC); China has twice been ruled by foreign dynasties; the country's present-day border disputes are only now being resolved, with the long border with India still heavily contested. The state has enshrined an uneasy, essentially colonial relationship with frontier peoples. It has done so through the establishment of "autonomous" regions, counties, and towns intended to provide a modicum of self-government and self-determination, through the creation of Minorities Institutes, which are universities and research centers that train minority elites while enshrining and studying local cultural traditions; and by providing preferential treatment in birth rates and designating spots for minorities in elite schools. Meanwhile, among the Han, minorities are often stereotyped as childlike, dirty, and exotic, unlike the official version, which shows China and its minorities as one big happy family. Woe to the ethnic minority group that seeks to challenge that narrative.

This chapter argues that the Chinese people are in essence in the throes of a crisis of identity, in which the nation is simultaneously well aware of its world prominence in past Imperial times and of its more recent humiliation at the hands of foreign powers from the mid-19th to mid-20th centuries. This dynamic can be understood, perhaps a bit crudely, as a "superiority-inferiority complex."

On the "superiority" side, there is a proud conviction that in prior millennia China was a great, unified Han civilization. China understood itself as the center of civilization, more advanced than other lands, a "Middle Kingdom" (the literal meaning of the Chinese characters for China, *zhongguo* 中国), where an emperor with the Mandate of Heaven to rule enjoyed tribute from other nations whose representatives traveled great distances to the Court to demonstrate their respect. This great Chinese civilization fostered the ancient philosophical traditions of Confucianism, Buddhism, and Daoism, among others, which articulated high moral values and offered prescriptions for achieving self-cultivation and a harmonious society. With regard to the non-human world, these traditions offered wisdom about the sustainable use of natural resources, reverence for all forms of life, and living in accordance with nature's flow (Weller 2006). Chinese are taught in school that they invented gunpowder, dynamite, the printing press, the compass, and paper, among thousands of other scientific innovations (all well chronicled by the great Sinologist Joseph Needham in his epic 27-volume work, *Science and Civilization in China*); their textbooks often start with the discovery of Peking Man as the first human being and key to a Marxist scientific outlook (Schmalzer 2008). Through their innovations in building complex waterworks projects, some of which survive to this day, the ancient Chinese harnessed nature by developing centralized political systems that facilitated social organization and flood control. The German Sinologist Karl Wittfogel (1957) even hypothesized, too simplistically perhaps, that the level of centralization required for such irrigation projects in "hydraulic societies" explains the emergence of the Chinese dynastic imperial system. Nonetheless, Yu the Great, the legendary founding emperor of the Xia Dynasty (about 2100 BC), is said to have gained his power and legitimacy by taming the waters during a great flood, cutting irrigation canals into the earth in place of failed dykes, and creating massive irrigation works, as in the historical tale, "Yu the Great controls the waters" [*Da Yu zhishui* 大禹治水]. In later years, Mao situated himself squarely within this tradition, building multiple dams and dreaming of blocking the Three Gorges on the Yangzi River. Mastery of nature has thus been a consistent part of the narrative of state power from pre-history, establishing a link between dynastic legitimacy and control of resources.

Most Chinese are ruefully aware, however, that somewhere along the way their great civilization lost this advantage, becoming known throughout the world as the "sick man of Asia," or as the founding father of modern China, Sun Yat-sen, famously put it in 1924, "a pile of loose sand," vulnerable to depredations and incursions of imperialist powers. This equally significant element of Chinese national identity thus tells the more recent history of humiliation at the hands of foreign powers. Indeed, the final dynasty, the Qing (1644–1911), was not Han but Manchu, a minority people from what is today Northeast China.

The events of the "centuries of humiliation" are sometimes treated as if they occurred yesterday. The Chinese were forced to import opium after the Opium Wars of the mid-19th century, with all the problems of dependency and addiction, because the trade was highly lucrative for the British and other foreign powers who exchanged opium for

Chinese tea. These wars were followed by a series of "unequal treaties" the Chinese were forced to sign in the 19th and early 20th centuries. Imposed by foreign powers after military defeat, they induced the Chinese to give up valuable land such as Hong Kong and Macao (to the British and Portuguese, respectively), to open their ports to foreign trade, to permit foreign missionaries to proselytize, and to allow foreign nationals to be subject not to Chinese law but to foreign legal systems while living in China. The centuries of humiliation included the Russian invasion of Manchuria in the Northeast in 1900 and the carving of the great city of Shanghai into colonial fiefdoms where elegant parts of town were off limits to Chinese. After the fall of the Qing dynasty in 1911, some of the unequal treaties with European colonial powers were abrogated. But the country descended into regional warlordism and a debilitating, multi-phase civil war between the Communists (CCP) and Nationalists (Kuomintang or KMT, or Guomindang or GMD depending on the Romanization system). This continued at a low level even during the invasion of China by Japan, the "rape" of the city of Nanjing in 1937, and the flight by both Nationalist and Communist armies toward the interior. When the Japanese were defeated in 1945, the civil war flared anew. Understandably, the Communist victory in 1949 was widely celebrated, with its promise of peace and prosperity. Mao's famous proclamation, as he stood on the reviewing stand at Tiananmen Square, "The Chinese people have stood up!" symbolized the passionate aspirations of the Chinese people.

A Communist Youth League instructor once lectured me for hours about the sins of foreign colonial powers. I had the misfortune to be berthed opposite him on an overnight train in Sichuan Province. He seemed to hold me personally responsible for the evils of my imperialist forebears, despite my protestations that I had not been born when any of these things happened, nor had my ancestors been involved. It was a good opportunity for me to see what every Chinese student is taught in mandatory "theory" and "Party history" classes in high school and university, and to understand why resentments toward foreigners may still lurk just beneath the surface of otherwise hospitable interactions.

Since those years of humiliation, China has struggled to reclaim what it regards as its rightful place at the center of the world. There is thus great sensitivity to indications of respect and rank. A preoccupation with "face" and status lies at the core of the tension between superiority and inferiority in Chinese national identity; the country's position in the eyes of the world is a primary concern for China and its citizens. This prickliness to questions of "face" arguably governs at least some of the country's international behavior. Memories of centuries of national humiliation at the hands of foreign powers can induce hair-trigger reactions to perceived slights (Gries 2005). Aggressive nationalism flares up easily, as is seen in competition with other nations for claims to ocean resources in the South China Sea or Sea of Japan, which China recently called a "core interest" along with Taiwan and Tibet.

This preoccupation underlay the delirium of national happiness when China was awarded the 2008 Olympics after many failed bids, and it helps explain the government's nervousness about air quality and the weather on opening night. So determined was the central government that the Olympics would mark China's great coming-out party on the world stage that it mobilized thousands of song and dance troupe members for years of preparation for the most lavish opening ceremonies in history and invested great sums to train athletes to win gold medals, even in sports where China had no prior tradition. The focus on reputation and status plays into China's desire to build the world's tallest, fanciest, most innovative and expensive buildings (architects adore receiving Chinese commissions, for it seems there is no limit on imagination or cost, and buildings like the Bird's Nest stadium have won prizes throughout the world). The Chinese are building the world's fastest trains, longest bridges, and most modern airports. The preoccupation with China's reputation contributes to the investment in the space program and the emphasis on putting a man on the moon, even at a time when rural children's parents struggle to pay school fees and Mao-era safety nets for workers and retirees are disappearing. National pride helps explain why China persisted in building the Three Gorges Dam at a time when developed countries were rethinking the wisdom of megaprojects which so dramatically alter the natural environment. "Face" also helps to explain why the Chinese reacted with outrage when in 1995 American environmentalist Lester Brown's book *Who Will Feed China?* raised concerns about global grain supply. The Chinese even published a rebuttal called "China Will Feed China," as if it were an insult to imply that China could not be self-reliant in grain (in fact, China's increasing reliance on the international grain market has had an impact on food prices which is being felt painfully in the world's poorest countries, as basic foodstuffs become increasingly expensive).

In international forums, sensitivity over "face" may explain why Chinese negotiators temporarily left the 2009 Copenhagen round of climate change negotiations in a huff when they discovered they had not been included in some side events, as well as the effort they put into placing a Chinese among the top officials at the International Monetary Fund when the arrest of Dominique Strauss-Kahn appeared to provide an opening at the top leadership (they won one of the number three spots). Preoccupation with face may also motivate some of China's behavior toward the Republic of China, Taiwan. China has provided generous aid to some of the world's smallest countries when they have agreed to renege on their recognition of Taiwan. China even blocked membership for Taiwan in the World Health Organization despite the fact that Taiwan, along with Hong Kong and Guangdong, was at the center of the major SARS virus outbreak in 2003. (Taiwan gained observer status at the WHO governing body in 2009.) The principle of a united China also plays a role in these efforts to regain past glory and reassert the Communist Party's defeat of the Kuomintang (KMT) once and for all. The return of Hong Kong to China from British rule in 1997 (one of the last vestiges of the unequal treaties) was marked with year-long, government-orchestrated celebrations, including performances, special souvenirs, lavish propaganda, and public demonstrations of apparently sincere patriotic joy.

CHINESE PHILOSOPHICAL TRADITIONS

Chinese identity is, of course, far more complex than a matter of face; indeed, to the extent that national culture usually involves some account of the human relationship to the non-human world, some Chinese environmentalists believe that traditional Chinese culture's elements of sustainability may provide important guidance during the current spiritual crisis of disillusionment and materialism. Their task is to create an ethical justification for a home-grown environmentalism that makes sense in the Chinese context and that does not simply appear to be a Western import intended to prevent China from developing, as is often suspected and suggested by government policy makers who do not subscribe to the emphasis on sustainability. All three major ancient traditions have such themes. Confucianism does so from an anthropocentric, or human-centered environmental perspective; Buddhism from a biocentric, or life-centered perspective; and Daoism from an ecocentric, or ecosystem-centered perspective (Weller 2006). Interestingly, Western environmental traditions have a similar range of philosophical approaches. The "stewardship" mandate of the Judeo-Christian tradition is human centered; the humane compassion of those who protect animals from cruelty and exploitation is rooted in reverence for the lives of all individual beings; the eco-centered land ethic guides conservation biologists and leads them to protect the world's "last great places," "critical eco-regions," "biogems," and "biodiversity hotspots" (in phrases used by the Nature Conservancy, World-Wide Fund for Nature, Natural Resources Defense Council, and Conservation International).

Many of China's ethnic minorities also have a history of stewardship and protection of the land. The Naxi minority, who number about 300,000 and live in Yunnan Province in Southwestern China, have a deep tradition of reverence for nature and a strict code that governs the use of water and harvesting of trees. Many of their forests were cut down during the Great Leap Forward and religious practices were banned during the Cultural Revolution. But some of the older people, while not religious, advocate respect for and balance with nature, based on traditional values. In one of the old ceremonies kept alive by religious leaders, prayers and offerings are made to the god of nature, asking to be forgiven for the damage to nature in daily life. If water and trees are not protected, it is believed, bad things such as floods, diseases, and crop failures will result.

In ancient China, as reflected in today's Communist Party's stated goal to achieve a "Harmonious Society," socio-political harmony in the human world was the most important social value. Orderly hierarchical relationships were bedrocks of the dominant Confucian tradition (and may underlie some of the preoccupation with respect and status described above). Such classics as the *Analects* teach moral qualities that promote both good leadership and loyalty. Rank and role, correctly performed, are the basis for social order. The correct performance of loyalty to one's superiors is amply repaid with paternalistic protection (Evasdottir 2004). Yet despite the focus on human relationships and such core values as filial piety, benevolence, ritual, morality, and loyalty [*xiao, ren, li, de, zhong* 孝,仁,礼,德,忠], Confucianism also provides sensible precepts protecting spawning fish and refraining from hunting in spring when animals are young. Raising freshwater prawn in rice paddies and carp in pools, as has been done in China for millennia, is often cited as one of the earliest examples of a sustainable and efficient farming system.

Chinese Buddhism (one of many schools of Buddhism, which is practiced differently in Sri Lanka, India, Tibet, Mongolia, Korea, Japan, and elsewhere), retains the notion of reincarnation of souls. Chinese Buddhist monks and nuns are often vegetarian, and many devout practitioners visit temples to have a vegetarian meal. On some festival days, Buddhists will purchase and release a bird, fish, or turtle as a way of gaining merit and as an acknowledgement of the connection among living beings and the desire to practice loving kindness to animals. There is thus a close relationship between nature and morality, with compassion to others held as one of the most important virtues.

Daoism, the most metaphysical of the three traditions, is famous for the saying, "the way that can be named is not the eternal way" [*dao ke dao, fei chang dao* 道可道，非常道]. It emphasizes the relationship between humans and the cosmos and sees man as a microcosm of nature, with the energetic *qi* [气], or life-force, flowing throughout the universe. Concepts of balance, the yin and the yang, and action through non-action are associated with this often-mystical school with many roots in folk traditions. Famously, the tradition discusses the power of *wuwei* [无为], or doing nothing. Compared with Confucianism and Buddhism, it most closely approximates ecological thinking, which also studies the flow of energy through ecosystems through the science of bioenergetics.

By contrast with these three ancient traditions, a fourth philosophical influence, more powerful by far, has come to dominate the developed world, including China, since the industrial revolution. Western-style modernization, which seeks to master nature through technological innovation, posits a separation between the human and non-human world and views nature as a force to be tamed. Some have seen this as an extension of a Judeo-Christian approach separating humans from nature, as articulated most famously in a 1967 essay by Lynn T. White, Jr., "The historical roots of our ecological crisis." In response to White's essay, some Christians plumbed the Bible for its environmental wisdom, using examples such as "Song of Songs" and the story of St. Francis of Assisi to find inspiration within the tradition (Hessel and Ruether 2000). In China, ironically, the modernization ethos received its starkest expression during the Maoist period, dominated by the slogan, "Man Must Conquer Nature" [*ren ding sheng tian* 人定胜天], which led to endless human suffering and destruction of wetlands and rainforests, and cast nature as an enemy to be humbled and punished (Shapiro 2001).

THE MAO YEARS AND THEIR LEGACY

Imperial decay, humiliation at the hands of foreign powers, warlordism, Japanese invasion, and civil war were followed in 1949 with the Communist victory, and patriotic Chinese returned to the mainland from around the world to build "New China." Children born during the first years of the revolution were told they were the luckiest people in the world (Liang and Shapiro 1983). But almost 30 years of political upheaval and human and natural catastrophe left China in dire straits. During the 1966–1976 Cultural Revolution, intense competition to be more revolutionary than the next person forced people to try to outdo each other in self-sacrifice and suffering. There were enormous political risks involved in any hint of "bourgeois" consumption; a person could be accused of bourgeois liberalism for growing a flower on a balcony, owning a cat or dog, or sitting on a padded chair. Meanwhile, Mao's campaigns to conquer nature felled forests to fuel makeshift steel furnaces, left forests denuded, and filled lakes and wetlands for ill-advised "Grain First" campaigns. Rivers were choked with the effluent of thousands of improperly sited and outfitted factories which had been relocated to the mountainous interior in the belief that they would be safer from aerial attack from the Russians. Urban "educated youth" were sent to China's border areas to prepare for war with the Soviet Union and Vietnam while remolding nature and themselves, while the professors and scholars who best understood the ecological value of biodiverse forests and wetlands were attacked as counter-revolutionaries and revisionists (Shapiro 2001). By the time of Mao's death in September 1976, China was isolated from much of the world, economically stagnant, and reeling from waves of political campaigns that had swept away the country's brightest, leaving survivors groping for ethical moorings.

The Chinese people then began to emerge from their long political and ideological nightmare. In December 1978, with the legendary Third Plenary Session of the 11th Chinese Communist Party Central Committee, reform-minded leaders such as Deng Xiaoping and Zhao Ziyang returned to power and endorsed a development program called the Four Modernizations (in agriculture, industry, defense, and science and technology), which opened China to the outside world after decades of isolation. Many of the new leaders had been victims of the Cultural Revolution who, when they were sent to the countryside in punishment for their "counter-revolutionary" ideas, saw firsthand how profoundly Mao's policies had failed the farmers. They launched a daring series of economic experiments to unleash the Chinese people's entrepreneurial initiative and to encourage their aspirations for better lives. Reforms spread gradually from rural areas to cities, where enterprises were made "responsible for their own profits and losses" rather than enjoying a guaranteed "iron rice bowl" of state support. With time, these reforms provided tremendous economic freedom, even to the point that China now seems more freewheelingly capitalistic than the West. Yet political reforms were limited, and village level elections were mostly pre-arranged until recent years. The Communist Party set policy, the national (State) government implemented it, and ordinary people had little ability to choose their leaders or their political system.

The Chinese people's desire for a better life after so much suffering, undergirded by their endless hard work and creativity, launched one of the greatest social transformations in history. A backlog of pent-up yearning for such basic creature comforts as upholstered furniture, wristwatches, bicycles, washing machines, and radios was gradually supplanted by a desire for status symbols and luxury goods. In an era of rising expectations and intense competition, materialism, and consumerism, the struggle for higher living standards and focus on the individual getting ahead replaced Mao-era slogans like "Serve the People" [*wei renmin fuwu* 为人民服务], which no longer carried weight. The Mao years left a legacy of corruption and disillusionment with the government which Chinese scholars and intellectuals have called a "crisis of confidence" [*xinyang weiji* 信仰危机] in public goals and values. The vacuum led people to cling to consumerism as a way to provide meaning to their lives and to be willing to tolerate a government which otherwise had betrayed them. There is much cynicism about public service or willingness to help anyone outside of personal networks, as seen during an October 2011 incident in Foshan in Guangdong Province, when passers-by failed to help a toddler who was struck by a vehicle, and then, when no one stopped to help her, was struck again and died. Public outrage and widespread discussion of the lack of compassion in Chinese national character followed in microblogs and Internet polls. Activist Dai Qing told the *New York Times'* Michael Wines (2011) that the passers-bys' callousness reflected a vacuum of beliefs: "All the traditional values of Chinese society were thrown out the window to make way for Mao and the rest of the party leadership. But that died long ago, and there was nothing to replace it except a materialistic hunger."

Whether environmental protection can ever become a shared public value under these circumstances is unclear (Bauer 2006). As far as environmental issues are concerned, there is an entrenched assumption, perhaps a legacy of the days when the government controlled all aspects of life, that even such public-spirited activities as cleaning trash from a river or from an apartment stairwell should be the job of the authorities. This attitude exacerbates tendencies to flout the law with respect to natural resources and/or pollution if so doing benefits oneself, one's family, and one's network of associates. (The melamine problem mentioned in previous chapters is a good example of this.) It also explains a tendency to litter which reached a peak in the 1990s; Wang Yongchen, a journalist and founder of Green Earth Volunteers, began her career filing stories about the massive amounts of garbage left by Chinese tourists visiting Lake Dianchi near Kunming.

Mistrust of Party and government leadership, and concomitant lack of respect for regulations and common goals, have if anything been intensified by a traditional culture which emphasizes personal relationships, obligations, and connections rather than rule of law. The post-Mao period has seen much waste of public assets and a culture of self-centeredness and desperation to succeed by any means. Frequent propaganda campaigns, and even executions of high-level officials for embezzlement and corruption, are aimed at stopping high officials' use of public funds for banquets, private cars, and brand name status symbols, but they seem to do little to change a national behavior pattern of wealth flaunting, self-interestedness, and disrespect for the law. Counterfeit currency, online scams, and fraudulent schemes abound at all levels of society. Moreover, the love of status symbols has fueled a huge market in fakes, creating a major international intellectual property headache and a cat-and-mouse effort to catch shipments of knockoff Gucci, Louis-Vuitton, Burberry, Coach, and North Face products at customs checkpoints. Meanwhile, in the impoverished interior and rural backwaters near wealthy areas, the desperately poor dream of taking their turn. Young people often join "floating populations" in the slums of the big cities and sweatshops in manufacturing hubs in the Southeast, leaving their hometowns all but empty of laborers. The massive influx of migrant workers returning home for Spring

Festival is an annual ritual that cripples the public transportation system.

A wonderful anecdote reported by Rebecca Marston of the BBC captures the focus on status of China's newly rich, as well as their emphasis on creating bonds of social obligation through generous gift-giving and sharing (2011). A group of wealthy businessmen were asked to bring their best bottles of imported wine to a gathering; some bottles cost as much as $1,600 apiece. They then poured them into a huge silver punchbowl and shared the contents as if they were so much sangria. (Other stories that cause oenophiles to have heart attacks describe fine wines mixed with orange soda or Coke.) This story captures the emphasis on face and wealth display, on collective life and the forging of the bonds of *guanxi* [关系, or mutually indebted personal connections], and on the brash crudeness of some of China's *nouveaux riches*. The Chinese love of status symbols has been a godsend for Louis Vuitton, which already makes 40 percent of its profit from Chinese buyers, for Gucci, with more than 40 stores in China, and for Burberry, Rolls Royce, Audi and other pricey brands. The Chinese are still trying to figure things out: I was once accosted by a young woman on the street in Chongqing wanting to know if "Malika" was a high status brand of cosmetics; she had just signed on to be a saleswoman. I eventually figured out she was talking about Mary Kay. As previously mentioned, McKinsey Insights China believes the country's luxury goods market could soon make up 20 percent of the global share, while CLSA Asia-Pacific Markets, a brokerage and investment firm, believes Chinese demand for luxury goods and travel could by 2020 account for 44 percent of global sales (2011).

The Chinese focus on status symbols may sometimes seem puzzling, but the recent history of war, hardship, and political upheaval explains some of the intensity of the huge unmet consumer demand. An awareness of the Chinese people's tribulations of the last century may provide a sympathetic context for current high levels of conspicuous consumption. However, it is sobering to consider the sharpening inequalities between rich and poor, coast and hinterland, for despite the high living standards of the middle and upper classes, millions of Chinese have yet to begin to satisfy their craving for consumption and wealth. According to the English-language official newspaper *China Daily*, the wealth gap between urban and rural Chinese is generally about 3.3 to 1, which Song Xiaowu, president of the China Society for Economic Reform, called an "appalling income disparity between the haves and have-nots" (Fu 2010). The sharp contrasts between rich and poor exacerbate the feeling of desperation among the poor and may contribute to the "me first" atmosphere that governs so many interactions. Migrant workers are motivated by "face" to send expensive gifts to their parents in the countryside and hide from them the harsh working conditions many of them endure in factories far from home, and are quick to seize on opportunities that appear to deliver a quick way out of poverty. So too are illegal immigrants in the West willing to endure tremendous privation and cruel working conditions in order to perform the Confucian duty of filial piety by sending home remittances and give their parents the "face" that comes with having offspring overseas.

As we see from the account above, China is engaged in a quest to reassert its historic great-power status, transforming urban landscapes, "conquering" nature with mega-projects, and engaging beyond its borders in ways designed to inspire notice and respect. Yet in the nationwide push for modernization, sustainability and social justice often fall by the wayside. During the past 30-plus years, China's economic growth and participation in global affairs have created some of the most dramatic social and economic changes ever to occur in a single country in such a short time; the prize of global respect is within reach. However, among the costs of such growth is some of the world's worst pollution, which threatens not only the people's health and well-being but also the country's image in the world and the government's legitimacy at home. The most dramatic example of China's drive to achieve a modernity designed to inspire the world's respect is undoubtedly the Three Gorges Dam.

The Three Gorges Dam has traditional roots in the longing for relief from natural disasters, an extension of the responsibility imperial leaders felt to tame the rivers that have so often brought the Chinese people sorrow. Indeed, the dam can be understood as a triumph of the national longing for flood control, although when it was approved many of the arguments centered on energy production. The dam was a dream of modern China's founding father Sun Yat-sen in the early 20th century, and celebrated further by Mao in this well-known anonymous translation of his famous poem:

> Great plans are afoot:
> A bridge will fly to span the north and south,
> Turning a deep chasm into a thoroughfare;
> Walls of stone will stand upstream to the West
> To hold back Wushan's clouds and rain
> Until a smooth lake rises in the narrow gorges.
> The mountain goddess, if she is still there
> Will marvel at a world so changed.

Only after Mao's death, however, did technocratic leaders – led by the widely disliked former engineer and then-Premier Li Peng – have the technical and financial confidence to go forward with the plan. When the dam was approved, opposition in the National People's Congress and among ordinary people was widespread. Resistance was especially fierce in the region above the dam, among the citizens and intellectuals of the huge industrial city of Chongqing, which stood to have its Mao-era factories with their residues of toxic heavy metals inundated and the swiftly flowing Yangzi turned into a stagnant catch-all for garbage and sewage. However, opposition could be expressed only passively: A 1992 vote taken by the Congress saw most people withholding the usual rubber-stamp of Party decisions by refraining from raising their hands. The prominent anti-dam activist, NPC member and former nuclear physicist and engineer Dai Qing, editor of two informative collections of essays about the risks of the dam, *Yangtze!,Yangtze!* (1994) and *The River Dragon has Come: The Three Gorges Dam and the Fate of China's Yangtse River and its People* (1998), was later imprisoned for a year, nominally for her support of the 1989 Tiananmen protests. Today, the dam stands as a monument to man's hubris and China's desire to obtain the admiration of the world. As predicted, it forcibly relocated more than two million people, was plagued with corruption and substandard construction and erosion, submerged rare archaeological structures, and likely dealt the last blow to the Yangzi River dolphin. Given their willingness to permit recent problems with the dam to be publicized, it is unlikely that the current group of Chinese leaders would have approved its current configuration, despite an official position which defends its flood control and electricity generation capacities. Nonetheless, small and large dams remain a critical part of China's plans to increase renewable energy percentages, despite frequent outcries about inadequate environmental impact assessments and siting on earthquake-prone grounds in the Far West, where much of China's unexploited hydropower potential lies. That a destructive project like the Three Gorges could be rammed through despite such widespread opposition gives little comfort to those concerned about some of the ambitious engineering efforts on the table today.

With little doubt, the modernization ethos, guided by the technocratic engineers who populate so many of the top echelons of China's Communist Party and state government, dominates and supersedes the traditions of Confucian sustainability, Buddhist reverence for life, and Daoist ecology. However, China's environmental problems do not lend themselves to a technological fix; they are political prob-

lems, social problems, and even problems of deep culture and philosophy. China's intellectuals understand the centrality of the culture
question, and indeed they have been wrestling with it for more than
100 years.

DEBATE ABOUT CHINESE CULTURE

An old conundrum for educated Chinese is whether Chinese culture
is stagnant, stifling, and feudalistic or the basis of a unique, harmonious, advanced, and superior Eastern civilization (Link 1992). During
the late Qing dynasty at the turn of the 20th century, there was a pro-
tracted public debate over which aspects of foreign culture could be
used to serve China – could China simply adopt the West's technology
or must it also import Western ideas? During the 1919 May Fourth
movement, a time of democratic expression and intellectual ferment,
young people consciously rejected Chinese feudalistic and paternalistic
social structures and embraced modern Western literature, lifestyles,
and political ideas. In the early 1920s, the novella, *The True Story of
Ah Q*, a masterpiece by Lu Xun, portrayed the Chinese people as
rationalizing their oppression and humiliation with infantilism, passivity, and self-deception. Much more recently, in 1988, the documentary
film maker Su Xiaokang took up some of the same themes in his six-
part series, "River Elegy" [*heshang* 河殤]. By portraying the traditional
symbol of Chinese greatness, the Great Wall, as a source of conserva-
tism and isolation and contrasting the invigorating "blue" seas of
modern foreign ideas with the dried-up culture of the Yellow River
(widely known as the cradle of Chinese civilization), he captured
Chinese intellectuals' deep ambivalence about Chinese tradition, so
often experienced as stultifying and insular, as compared with fresh
ideas from the outside world. The political sensitivity of this critique
of traditional Chinese culture, which preceded the 1989 Tiananmen
demonstrations which were the greatest threat to the power of the

Chinese Communist Party since their victory in 1949, resulted in the filmmaker being driven into exile in the U.S. and to an organized nationwide criticism and denunciation of the film's ideas.

The ongoing vitality and urgency of the debate over national identity is reflected in the enormous popularity of Jiang Rong's 2008 semi-autobiographical novel, *Wolf Totem* (published in 2004 as *Lang Tuteng* 狼图腾 in Chinese), which sold so many copies in China that only the little red book, *Quotations from Chairman Mao*, has sold more. The lead character is a Han Chinese "sent down" to Inner Mongolia in the 1960s, where he learns the secrets of indigenous knowledge about the relationship between wolves and the grasslands ecosystem and then witnesses how Han culture destroys that balance. Settlers eradicate the wolves that keep the gazelles in check. They destroy the grasslands and the creatures that live on it by turning them into farmland. Weak and passive Han culture is contrasted with the wild courage of the Mongol herdsmen (connected to that of the wolf), and thus the novel becomes an indictment of Han Chinese passivity as compared with the courage of the meat-eating, wolf-like natives. It is an elegy for the ethnic minority culture, grasslands, and the creatures destroyed wantonly by Han bureaucrats and settlers.

Nowadays, variations of the same debate continue as a quiet struggle rages over China's national identity. There are unresolved questions about the legacy of the Mao period, doubts about the legitimacy of the Chinese Communist Party, and competing visions of the country's guiding values and goals. This discussion takes place at the margins of social, political, and intellectual life, expressed indirectly in the press and academic studies because a full airing of the issues might call the government's legitimacy into question. Yet its implications for China's development are enormous. The value placed on "face" sometimes leads a country to make ill-considered judgments about the use of national funds, as occurred when so much money was spent on the Three Gorges Dam and is now being spent on space exploration, when China would be better served by investing in improving the lot of the poor. But there is hope that the narrative of sustainability may yet become strong enough to guide China's development decisions.

China's people face a long list of questions about their identity; both the government and the newly ambitious citizenry have some soul-searching to do. Is China to look to the past and reconnect with its heritage of civility, respect for the ancient and pragmatic understanding of the value of sustainable management practices? Is China to focus on the present moment as it builds wealth and power and expends its energies on material success? Is China to look toward the future to become an innovator in the search for new models of sustainable development and a leader in global citizenship? How are the Chinese people to understand their history and destiny, with memories of past humiliations so vivid, and nagging suspicions that flaws in national culture and character may have contributed to the country's suffering and may yet presage future disasters? How is China's government to deal with the painful legacy of the Cultural Revolution and the Tiananmen massacre, and with the enormous pressures of exploding consumption demands and mounting environmental problems? These questions recur as the Chinese struggle to find guidance through the environmental quagmire: Does the answer lie in the Confucian tradition of harmony between the heavens – often understood as nature – and man [*tian-ren heyi* 天人合一] as a way of building social stability? Is it in the Buddhist tradition of reverence for life? Or perhaps in the Daoist "Way" of accommodating nature and going with the flow? Or, as contemporary policy makers seem to believe, in a blend of Maoist and capitalist modernization and nature conquest? Is the solution to "return to the roots" as seen in the fashion for things Tibetan and rural, or to turn outwards to the West and adopt the ethos of the global environmental movement? Do Chinese ideas of nature provide most guidance, or those of foreign environmentalists? Does the answer lie with the individual or the collective? Discussions of many of these questions are nascent, but the government's fear of organized groups and its desire to control the official version of China's recent history, particularly the Cultural Revolution, acts as a deterrent to a full and open national dialogue.

As we have seen in this chapter, the Chinese people seem at times to swing between jingoism, or pugnacious nationalism, and insecurity or what a psychologist might call "low self-esteem." Every interaction with outsiders is the more sensitive because it is scrutinized for evidence of China's relative status. Traditions that emphasize social hierarchy, which are also very much alive in other Confucian societies like Taiwan, Japan, and Singapore, have become exaggerated as China flexes its muscles in international politics. The deep-rooted concern for "face" has colored China's development decisions, leading the government to put resources into tangible, image-building achievements, coupled with efforts to reach out internally and internationally to guarantee supplies of energy, grain, and raw materials and "pacify the borders" once and for all. Often, such decisions are detrimental to social needs. Nevertheless, there are signs that an alternative model of development is also emerging. There is more discussion of sustainable development at the top levels of Chinese leadership than in almost any Western country. Incentives for industry to create "green" jobs and innovations are significant. The stalled effort to establish an annual "Green GDP" to evaluate the environmental costs of economic development may be revived. The stringent automobile fuel efficiency standards are a credit to the nation. Reconsideration of plans to build multiple dams on the pristine Nu River and Upper Yangzi in Yunnan may reduce their number and degree of impact. There is thus a possibility that China's preoccupation with "face" and national identity may yet be channeled in support of an alternative model that the world has not yet seen. Of course, there is no simple, direct causal relationship between attitudes and beliefs, on the one hand, and behavior and policy on the other; a solid environmental education for all children and public promotion of "green" values would not be sufficient to shift China or the world onto a less damaging path. However, they may be necessary first steps. China may be able to resolve its environmental crisis using techno-logical leapfrogging and courageous policy making to become a global leader in truly sustainable development. For this transformation to succeed, however, a national dialogue and effort to promote a "green" national identity, and to engage and empower public participation and civil society, will be required.

QUESTIONS FOR RESEARCH AND DISCUSSION

1 To what extent do you think that Chinese attitudes and beliefs shape behavior and policy with respect to interaction with the non-human world? Are teaching values of sustainability and strong sci-entific training about the costs of global resource depletion and pollution necessary to shift human interactions with non-human nature in China? Is your response the same or different for your own country?

2 How does China's history affect its citizens' attitudes toward China's role in the world? How might that history affect China's prospects for sustainable development? Can you discuss this question for your own country?

3 Given the Chinese people's recent history of privation, can the world expect anything different than the new culture of conspicuous con-sumption? How would you react if other nations or even your own government told you not to aspire to a better material living stan-dard? What *is* a better living standard?

4 How is Chinese national identity different from yours? How is it similar? Can you identify an environmental issue where you could find common ground with Chinese attitudes? Is there any evidence

in your country of an emerging sustainability ethic that rejects a materialistic and consumerist ideology of modernization?

ADDITIONAL RESOURCES

- Jayshree Bajoria, Council on Foreign Relations, April 23, 2008, "Nationalism in China," http://www.cfr.org/china/nationalism-china/p16079
- Forum on Religion and Ecology (Yale University), at: http://www.yale.edu/bioethics/FORE.htm
- Orville Schell, "China: Humiliation and the Olympics," July 2008. Available on the *New York Review of Books* website.
- Lu Xun, *The True Story of Ah Q* (1921), Marxists Internet Archive, at: http://www.marxists.org/archive/lu-xun/1921/12/ah-q/index.htm

5   Public Participation and Civil Society: The View from Below

Chinese civil society faces severe limitations in its ability to organize, communicate, and conduct activities. Yet even as there are tremendous changes with respect to the environment from the top down, as well as new demands for pollution controls and food safety from influential middle class consumers, the grass roots are feeling their power and becoming active, often forming a partnership with the upper reaches of the bureaucracy in order to pressure corrupt developers, self-interested local officials, lower- and middle-level bureaucrats and polluting factory operators. Almost all citizens' groups cultivate ties with top leaders and agencies as a form of protection and assurance that they have a green light for their activities.

It is important not to over-generalize about Chinese civil society, for China is a large, diverse, and unevenly developed country, with unequal distribution of resources and local empowerment. The eastern seaboard and urban areas have different characteristics and dynamics than rural areas and interior western provinces. Nonetheless, even in remote areas such as the Nu River region near Myanmar and the Upper Yangzi near the Tibetan Autonomous Region, there are signs of an increasingly vibrant civil society; environmental activists and filmmakers have helped to educate and inspire local people to oppose a series of dams that would displace them. Moreover, as we will see in the next chapter, some of the less developed regions such as Tibet and Yunnan are also hothouses of biodiversity and inhabited by ethnic minority nationality people who often have political reasons for resisting the dominance of the Han. This combination contributes to environmental activism in remote areas where it might not be expected and draws the attention of urban elites intent on intervening in dam projects and resource extraction that degrade landscapes and threaten biodiversity. However, because of the politically sensitive combination of minority populations and resources problems, the government often construes such environmental activism as ethnic unrest.

Not all Chinese public participation is expressed through citizens' groups. Complaint hotlines provide government-organized safety valves for individuals to register discontent with polluting factories (Brettell 2008). Moreover, "environmental mass incidents," as the government calls such protests, are astonishingly numerous. In some cases, public participation is fueled by localized pollution such as that which causes "cancer villages" and arises spontaneously, through cell-phone messaging and social media such as *weibo*, the Chinese version of Twitter. In other cases, NGO activists lead the way to greater citizen participation by conducting information sessions and providing advice and legal support.

Despite such new opportunities, there is continued repression of environmental activists and ordinary citizens, who face monitoring, detention, or imprisonment because of their protests. Information may be censored, activist groups are watched, and there can be heavy penalties for unsanctioned public assembly. Even top environmental officials' candid statements about China's dire environmental conditions and the need for more transparency of information about pollution, such as those made by former environment ministry spokesman Pan Yue, may carry political risks: Pan Yue's vivid descriptions of the severity of air and water pollution in China, his proposal for more democratic participation by ordinary people to fight pollution, and his criticisms of polluting industries and local officials, which were widespread in 2007, have in recent years become muted and a Green GDP project that he championed has at least temporarily been shelved.

This chapter presents a snapshot of China's emerging environmental civil society. It profiles leading NGOs and activists. It explores the framework in which organizations exist, including the role of government-organized NGOs (GONGOs) and think tanks. It also presents trends in environmental activism, including new pressures for transparency about air and water pollution, the increase in NGO- and citizen-initiated lawsuits, and growing confidence in the rule of law.

In China, citizens' groups (non-governmental organizations) are classic illustrations of the Gramscian argument that civil society is often penetrated by the state as a way of manipulating culture to gain consent for government rule. The Communist Party issued regulations regarding groups as a priority immediately after the 1949 revolution, in the form of Interim Procedures on the Registration of Social Organizations. From the very beginning, the Chinese government viewed independent social organizations as potential threats to the governance of the Communist Party. Under the 1950 registration measures, most social organizations were suppressed as feudal or reactionary organizations, while the few that survived were subsumed into the government system or transformed into government affiliates.

During the Mao years, and especially during the 1966–1976 Cultural Revolution, independent social organizations simply could not exist: Aside from Communist mass organizations such as the Young Pioneers, Communist Youth Leagues, and neighborhood associations that were effectively decentralized monitoring networks to allow the Party to keep tabs on citizens, any other social group was treated as counter-revolutionary, and its leaders denounced. Although the ultra-leftist, often fascist Red Guard organizations had, arguably, their elements of public participation and democratic expression, the period was marked by extreme violence toward religious groups, artists and writers, educated people of all persuasions, and anyone with foreign ties. Dictatorship, anarchy, chaos, and economic stagnation marked the decade. The Party itself was wracked with internecine struggles, creating one of the most vicious and tumultuous periods in human history.

After Mao died and Deng Xiaoping came into power with his economic reforms and modernization platform, more space became available for individual expression, freedom of information, and participation in unofficial social groups. From 1979 to 1989, the number of national-level social organizations increased 16-fold, reaching an official figure of 1,600. Local social organizations increased 33-fold during the same period, reaching 200,000. New policies were issued in the late 1980s, including the Regulations on Registration and Administration of Social Organizations (RRASO) and Regulations for the Management of Foundations (RMF). According to these policy documents, a social organization had to be authorized by a government agency supervisor in order to be legally registered. Social groups have nicknamed their supervisor their "mother-in-law." Registration is very difficult, because most governmental agencies are hesitant to take responsibility for the behavior of a citizens' group. Having a supervisory body undermines the independence of social organizations, so some organizations register as business entities, while many more operate underground without legal identities, such as the illegal pro-Vatican Catholic Church and various human rights and democracy groups. In 1998 and 2004, amendments were made to RRASO and RMF, respectively, while Provisional Regulations for the Registration Administration of People-Run Non-Enterprise Units were issued in 1998. However, registration for social organizations did not become any easier. By 2010, 440,000 social organizations were registered in China, while around 3 million or more organizations remained unregistered, meaning that almost 90 percent of these groups could not have a bank account under the organization's name or enjoy other perquisites such as tax breaks. This lack of financial recognition complicates their ability to receive donations and makes their activities expensive.

Moreover, religious groups and the military remain prohibited from forming such organizations, a reflection of the central government's nervousness about challenges to its rule. Historically, dynasties have been shaken by millennial groups such as the White Lotus Society and the Taipings, which may explain the government's sensitivity to the popular Falungong religious sect.

Timothy Hildebrandt, a scholar of Chinese civil society, describes the difficulty of coming up with reliable statistics about the number of NGOs. He writes in an email, "One option would be to cite 'officially registered' organizations. According to the Ministry of Civil Affairs, in 2008, that was 220,000. The big problem is that a large proportion of NGOs are not registered at all, or if they are legally registered, it is as businesses – do those count?" Hildebrandt's work suggests that more environmental NGOs are registered than NGOs involved in other social issues, although the smaller ones are not registered. He mentions another problem: What counts as an NGO? Those which self-identify as such? Those which formally register? Those which engage only in non-profit projects? Those which have more than one person on staff? Moreover, local governments that once welcomed the work of ENGOs no longer do so. This is largely due to changing interests which favor economic development projects which might often be opposed by these very ENGOs. These factors have taken a toll on the proportion of environmental groups in the larger universe of Chinese NGOs. In Yunnan, when Hildebrandt consulted a directory of NGOs that had been compiled just a couple of years prior to his arrival in 2009, more than 70 percent of those organizations listed no longer existed (personal communication 2011). Increased restrictions on accepting foreign money were no doubt a factor, as well as provincial-level scrutiny of some groups seen as obstructing state dam-building goals for energy production. So, with the growth in the scope of civil society organizations in China, coupled with waning funding for environmental groups, the proportion of ENGOs has diminished, even if, in terms of number of organizations, there are more ENGOs today than 15 years ago.

Despite these difficulties, NGO registration policy seems to be easing in some cities in recent years, especially for pilot projects. In 2008, Shenzhen opened up registration for social organizations in the fields of social welfare and charity, and in July 2011, Minister of Civil Affairs Li Liguo announced that the whole country would adopt a similar social organization registration policy. Such groups are now supposed to be able to register directly with civil affairs departments, and supervisory bodies will no longer be needed (*China Daily* 2011a). However, the situation for environmental NGOs remains fraught with challenges and the details of the more permissive registration system have yet to be worked out in practice.

MODES OF POLITICAL PARTICIPATION

In Western debates over civil society advocacy groups, some "realist" scholars argue that non-governmental organizations do not matter much in shaping world events; the unitary state is the main actor in both domestic and international affairs. However, an increasingly large and influential group of scholars sees such groups as wielding power and participating in governance. Civil society organizations control information, shape behavior, serve as consultants to governments, influence consumer choices and power, and exert pressure by bearing witness to the actions of corporations and governments and holding them accountable. The groups link across state borders in "global civil society" such that at times they do not seem firmly fixed within one state or another, forming alliances and commitments to causes that transcend traditional state boundaries (Wapner 1995). Moreover, there is a rich relationship between environmental activism and the development of civil society in general. Given that in China civic groups that focus on human rights and democracy are quickly suppressed, some activists have found the "space" for organizing around environmental issues to be attractive. As a result, active and creative people who wish to engage in public participation have sometimes turned to that area. Some international scholars have invested great attention to environmental groups as a way of measuring the potential for democratic change in the country more broadly; some of this interest comes from rightwing academics interested in seeing whether the power of the Chinese Communist Party is weakening or on the verge of collapse (Diamond 2009).

While a detailed discussion of the scholarly debates about NGOs is too complex to present here, it may be helpful to consider some of the sources of power available to citizens' groups. One useful typology comes from Margaret Keck and Kathryn Sikkink (1998), who identify several basic modes of NGO engagement, among which the politics of information, accountability, and symbolism are the most relevant for the Chinese case. "Information politics," the historically earliest and most traditional form of NGO power, comes into play when a group gathers and disseminates information via newspapers, magazines, and other media. For example, conservation groups which conduct or convey to the public the results of scientific research about threats to specific species such as the Tibetan antelope, or groups that have information about pollution coming from certain factories, derive power and influence simply by publicizing that material. Chinese journalists have demonstrated a powerful interest in environmental stories and have often become advocates for justice in cases of pollution, poorly designed and constructed dams, and threats to wildlife. Moreover, Chinese ENGOs have increasingly turned to citizen and consumer survey research as one source of their power, publicizing their findings on websites and via social media but also partnering with official think tanks and governmental agencies to make their findings known.

"Accountability politics" involves holding governments and corporations accountable to commitments they have made in public forums such as the U.N., or in treaties they have signed and ratified, or in corporate mission statements, or adherence to codes of conduct that they have endorsed. Chinese ENGOs are increasingly joining forces with citizens' groups around the world in this effort. For example, in collaboration with an international ENGO, TRAFFIC, they monitor compliance with the 1973 Convention on International Trade in Endangered Species (CITES) in an effort to force the government to deal with the illegal wildlife trade that is rampant in public markets throughout the country. Although CITES cannot address domestic consumption of endangered species because that is a matter of national sovereignty, the treaty restricts the import and export of such creatures and as such is one of the only weapons such groups have available. Human rights NGOs have long used accountability politics to try to pressure the Chinese government since China has associated itself with 22 international human rights treaties, including the Universal Declaration on Human Rights, the U.N. Covenant on Economic and Social Rights, and the key U.N. Covenant on Civil and Political Rights (which China has signed but not ratified). Among the environmental treaties that China has signed, CITES is highly relevant for Chinese citizens' groups, along with the 1989 Basel Convention on the Control of Transboundary Wastes and their Disposal. Moreover, Chinese citizens' groups are increasingly engaged in pressuring their government on climate change, and Chinese NGOs were an active presence in Copenhagen, Cancun, and Durban, where governments were negotiating an extension or revamping of the soon-to-expire Kyoto Protocol.

Finally, "symbolic politics" uses images, media, and dramatization techniques to mobilize opposition or consumer behavior. Greenpeace International, with its Quaker roots in "bearing witness," specializes in this technique, made famous when it used inflatable boats to confront giant factory whaling ships and videotaped the vulnerability of the whales and the heroism of its activists. Social media have become even more powerful tools of political power for NGOs through new techniques of membership drives, petitions, and blogging. For example, a Greenpeace-China campaign was designed to pressure Nike and Adidas to remove hazardous chemicals from their supply chains so as to stop polluting the Yangzi River. Greenpeace members were asked to "Sign the petition to tell Nike and Adidas to Detox Now!" After Puma and Nike caved in to consumer pressure, an August 2011 email campaign intensified the focus on Adidas:

> We began the Detox campaign in June with a "Nike vs Adidas" challenge, but Puma was first off the mark with its commitment to eliminate all hazardous chemicals from its supply chain and products. Nike last week committed too, leaving people to wonder what Adidas thinks about its customers and the environment. According to China's *Statistical Yearbook*, the apparel, footwear and caps textile industry discharge 805 tonnes of industrial waste water every second. Our latest Dirty Laundry report reveals that the clothes in your local sportswear or fashion outlet may contain nonylphenolethoxylates, which break down in water to form nonylphenol – a toxic, persistent and hormone-disrupting chemical.

Later that month, Adidas announced that it too would commit to zero discharge of toxic chemicals.

Corporations know that if they are perceived as environmentally friendly they will gain buyers, but if they become negative targets this can have a serious impact on their bottom lines. This is a concern for multinational corporations that manufacture in China, not only because they tend to export to places where Greenpeace and other environmental NGOs have strong voices, but also because an increasingly large percentage of their sales are to domestic consumers who are paying attention.

FRIENDS OF NATURE

One of the earliest and most famous Chinese environmental NGOs was founded in 1993 (and officially registered in 1994) by Liang Congjie, who passed away in 2010. His remarkable story is worth telling. Liang Congjie was the grandson of the great early 20th century reformer-journalist Liang Qichao, who was the inspiration and leader, together with Kang Youwei, of the 1898 Hundred Days Reform and an advocate of constitutional monarchy in the waning days of the Qing dynasty. Exiled to Japan and later a lecturer in the U.S., Liang Congjie's grandfather met Theodore Roosevelt and tried to stimulate in China an interest not only in Western technology but also in Western forms of political organization. Associated with the revered "father of the nation" Sun Yat-sen, he is known today as a reformer rather than as a revolutionary. His reputation as one of the great figures in the history of modern China is unassailable.

Liang Qichao's son, Liang Sicheng (the environmentalist Liang's father), was a famed and then persecuted architectural preservationist. After the Mao revolution, Liang Sicheng fought tirelessly, if ultimately fruitlessly, to save Beijing's ancient city walls from demolition and to chronicle the forms and styles of Chinese architecture that were endangered and being lost. Yet during the Cultural Revolution, Liang Sicheng was viciously victimized for what were considered his reactionary ideas about preserving the artifacts of feudal society. According to his wife, whom I met in 1983, during his final days he was held prisoner in a damp cellar where water sometimes rose to his waist. He was made to bow and apologize to his tormentors, who sometimes urinated through the cellar window to humiliate him. He was eventually "persecuted to death," like so many others of China's greatest and brightest, in a period of extremism and violence from which China has yet to recover or fully to understand.

After the Cultural Revolution, Liang Sicheng's reputation was posthumously rehabilitated and his greatness widely acknowledged. His son Liang Congjie, who had also suffered during the Cultural Revolution, was treated with the respect accorded to China's greatest public intellectuals. This heritage provided him with a unique level of political protection, and helps explain how he was able to take risks at a time when the regime treated civil society groups with great suspicion.

When I first met Liang Congjie in the early 1980s, he had regained access to his family's traditional Beijing home after it had been confiscated, and was working as an encyclopedia publisher and translator. Even then, Liang Congjie was deeply worried about environmental issues, but knew that the confrontational techniques used by international groups would be too dangerous to use in China. But he had the vision, and the political protection, to establish Friends of Nature together with a small group of other intellectuals concerned about the environment. His pedigree gave them the freedom to do what others could not, and his sophisticated awareness of the risks allowed them to navigate a sensitive situation. As a result of his early courageous efforts, Liang is widely recognized as the father of the Chinese NGO environmental movement.

One of the causes considered politically safe in the early days was the effort to save the Tibetan antelope, or *chiru*, whose underbelly fur is highly sought for making scarves called shatoosh, said to be so fine that they can be pulled through a finger ring. Many of the poachers are ethnic minorities and the fur is generally smuggled to India for sale in the West, so the Chinese central government apparently had no problem with this campaign. Still, it was dangerous, and two Tibetan wildlife officials were killed during the 1990s for their efforts to stop poachers: Suonan Dajie died in a gunfight; his brother-in-law Zhaba Duojie, was murdered in his home four years later.

One activity of Friends of Nature was to bring environmental education directly into towns and villages in a car decorated like an antelope. But a more significant aspect of the *chiru* campaign was its role in creating networks of environmentalists throughout the country. In the 1990s, saving the antelope became one of several causes that lent itself to Internet organizing, and the effort spread to universities throughout the country, thereby contributing to the formation of student groups, which often conducted activities under the aegis of the Communist Youth League as approved clubs. These networks became an important source of information exchange and organizing ability for China's environmental movement with respect to other topics. Eventually, Liang Congjie achieved global recognition by being awarded the 2000 Ramon Magsaysay award for public service, which stated:

> In the highly centralized political society of China, Liang has drawn attention to ecological issues where it matters most – in the center. And by choosing his causes carefully and working closely with certain national and local officials, he has avoided the pitfall of alienating government, still China's most powerful force for change. But by scrupulously maintaining FON's independence, Liang has also demonstrated the critical role that nongovernmental organizations can play in addressing China's urgent public concerns (http://www.rmaf.org.ph/Awardees/Citation/CitationLiangCon.htm).

Liang Congjie was a dignified, humble, and dedicated person. He told me on numerous occasions how difficult it was to run the organization. He feared it would be shut down if he went too far, and voluntarily limited membership to 10,000 in order not to appear threatening to central authorities. Still, he needed to find activities for Friends of Nature's passionate members. Unlike in the West, where environmental organization members often write a check and receive a magazine, umbrella, calendar, or tote bag in return, Chinese members expect to participate actively, perhaps a legacy of Mao-era mobilization campaigns where people were organized for mass activities like building small dams or killing "pests" like rats and mosquitoes. Membership was not automatic; candidates had to write a letter to the organization explaining why they wanted to join. Liang and his small staff then organized trips for volunteers to plant trees, pick up garbage, and conduct other activities that the government would not find threatening. Liang also translated or arranged to have translated numerous environmental books by Western writers. This publication effort eventually blossomed into Friends of Nature's annual publication of the *China Environment Yearbook*, in cooperation with the Chinese Academy of Social Sciences Press, which presents a collection of views of the year's challenges from an NGO perspective. Also translated into English, the volumes offer insight into everything from legal challenges against poorly planned dams to the Green GDP effort to overviews of the year in environment from the perspective of NGO leaders (2007–2011).

Since those early days, many environmental groups have formed, but Friends of Nature paved the way. It served as an incubator for numerous other environmentalists who then went on to form their own groups, such as that of the famous photographer and journalist couple Xi Zhinong and Shi Lihong, who worked to try to save the Yunnan snub-nosed monkey in Deqin, China's "Shangri-la," filming the illegal logging that was destroying monkey habitat and moving their young family to that remote region. Xi's photos of the monkeys have become icons of the Chinese environmental movement, and he and his wife have continued to write and make films about other environmental causes like the planned dams on the Nu River and Tiger Leaping Gorge, using their organization Wild China as a platform. Other well-known groups include Sherri Liao Xiaoyi's Global Village-Beijing, which promotes recycling and a "green" lifestyle and produces early childhood environmental films. Winner of the 2000 Norwegian Sophie

Prize, Liao Xiaoyi studied for a time in the West and became familiar with American forms of activism, but for many years could not find a "mother-in-law" for her organization, so she registered as a small business and paid heavy taxes (she finally registered a few years ago). Outside Beijing, well-known groups include Green Han River, which was founded by "environmental grandma" Yun Jianli, and Green Camel Bell in Gansu, established by Zhao Zhong to protect the environment in the Lanzhou area. This limited list does not begin to account for the numerous environmental student clubs and other green groups that have become so fashionable among young people worried about the state of China's environment and eager to join a global movement for protection.

Many of the leading environmental activists in China today were originally journalists. They were the first to explore and expose the devastating pollution that has left nearly half of the population without a supply of clean water and a third breathing polluted air. Shi Lihong originally wrote for *China Daily*, her husband Xi Zhinong was once a cameraman for China Central Television. Investigative environmental journalist Liu Jianqiang was a leading reporter for the influential *China Southern Weekend*. Ma Jun wrote *China's Water Crisis*, a journalistic exposé of the pollution of the Yellow River, before founding the Institute for Public and Environmental Affairs (IPE), which publishes information released by the Ministry of Environmental Protection about polluting factories. As already described, Ma Jun has used this website to pressure international corporations like athletic shoe manufacturers to clean up their suppliers in China. The close relationship between the IPE and the MEP, wherein the government produces reports detailing polluters and the IPE advances the political campaign to effect change, justifies Qu Geping's view that environmental NGOs should be encouraged. They are, he has said, "another arm of the government" that can help to monitor the environment from the bottom up.

Not all government officials take such a benign view of ENGOs. In Yunnan Province an NGO founded by social scientist Yu Xiaogang, Green Watershed, clashed with local officials over the environmental and social impact of the construction of dams. Yu gathered and circulated evidence that farmers on the Mekong River (Lancang in China) had been poorly compensated when they were forced off their land. When Yu and filmmaker Shi Lihong made and circulated a documentary about the abject poverty of the former farmers, it stirred up resistance to a series of major dams proposed for Yunnan. Local officials who favored the dams, even at the cost of displacing another 150,000 people, became alarmed. Yu was questioned and his organization threatened. But the plight of the farmers reached the national press and Premier Wen Jiabao himself began to urge caution in the development of dams. The local government was pressured to better compensate the farmers on the Lancang and this took pressure off Yu.

Yu's organization went on to build a ten-year demonstration project in a group of Naxi villages in central Yunnan Province. With support from international NGOs like Oxfam and the Nature Conservancy, Green Watershed helped local farmers to form cooperatives to reforest areas devastated during the Cultural Revolution and to manage the fishing in the nearby lake. They installed solar hot water heaters as well as biogas generators to provide cooking gas from pig manure and human waste. Yu's hope is that by showing how health and wealth can be increased and carbon dioxide production and pollution diminished in one watershed, he will inspire similar work elsewhere.

This process, whereby ENGOs take the initiative, the central government provides legitimacy, and the media reports the results, has created a fragile but useful model for environmental groups. How far this model can go, however, is questionable because of basic limitations placed on ENGOs. Environmental groups may be more easily tolerated than the democracy movement, but they are not allowed to have national chapters and cannot advertise to raise funds. The limited funds that they do raise come from patrons and members, and from project funds provided by international NGOs. Until the government relaxes the limitations on funding and national organizing, and signals that it is willing to permit the existence of much larger ENGOs, the impact of the green movement will be limited. But even with these restrictions, many of these activists have become household names. Xi Zhinong, the wildlife photographer who defended the adorable snub-nosed monkeys of Yunnan, is a frequent guest on television shows where he is asked his opinions about everything from air conditioners to electric cars. His and his wife Shi Lihong's films have been screened at international wildlife film festivals, and many of the activists have studied or been invited as guest lecturers at universities and think tanks worldwide. Government officials like Pan Yue and Qu Geping have long advocated for loosening constraints and to allow more people to mobilize. The environment is a perfect area to explore greater democracy, they argue, because it does not undermine the political system and it is relatively easy to reach consensus on the desirability of environmental protection.

GOVERNMENT-ORGANIZED NGOs (GONGOs)

In addition to ENGOs founded by intellectuals, grassroots environmental activists, and students, ENGOs established by governmental agencies and governmental officials also play an important role in international environmental cooperation, environmental education, and environmental campaigns. Such groups can play a very positive role for the environment, for the reality is that Chinese political life takes its cues from the central government and the central government is far from monolithic. Such GONGOs are often strong, independent voices for environmental protection from within the government (Wu, Fengshi 2002).

Among top-down organized and funded GONGOs, one of the largest is the All-China Environment Federation, founded in

2005 under the patronage of the State Environmental Protection Administration (now Ministry of Environmental Protection). The SEPA website describes it as a non-profit national social organization, but we can easily see the close governmental ties in its mandate:

The Federation aims to implement the strategy of sustainable development, achieve the goal of environment and development as set out by the State, and to safeguard the environmental interests of the public and the society. The major tasks are to keep contacts with influential and high-profile senior personages, unite a variety of social groups, and play the role of solidarity and coherence; put forward proposals on government environmental decision-making; provide services on environmental laws for the public and the society; enable the public and the society to get access to environmental information, and conduct activities for environmental publicity and education; promote the sound development of China's environmental NGOs and help them build and obtain their due position in international communities; and undertake other work as entrusted by the government and relevant organizations.

Another prominent GONGO is the China Environmental Protection Foundation (CEPF), which was established by Qu Geping, the first Administrator of SEPA, whose book on China's population we have already mentioned. The organization can be traced to the seminal 1992 U.N. Conference on Environment and Development in Rio de Janeiro, Brazil, where he shared the $100,000 UNEP Sasakawa Prize for his contributions in promoting and supporting environmental protection in China. In accepting the award, Qu Geping proposed to use it to establish a fund for environmental work in China. One year later, with support from SEPA and other central governmental agencies, the CEPF was established to raise funds for environmental protection, facilitate environmental cooperation between China and other countries, and issue grants for environmental projects. Most board members of the CEPF have governmental backgrounds and, like the All-China Environment Federation, the CEPF's supervisory body is the Ministry of Environmental Protection, which elects board members and supervises the work. However, the CEPF has autonomy over its daily operations and projects. It has awarded individuals and organizations that have made prominent contributions to environmental protection the China Environment Prize since 2000, and funded numerous environmental projects, such as the Ecology Great Wall project, which supports tree planting and sustainable agricultural programs in rural northwest China.

There are also striking examples of the government working directly with local villages to restore ecosystems that have been devastated by poor farming practices stretching back for centuries. On the Loess Plateau north of the Yellow River in Central China, the silted soil once supported lush forests, but overgrazing and overly intensive farming turned the region into an eroded, barren landscape. With support from the World Bank, the central government intervened to work slowly and carefully with villagers in an area the size of Belgium, hiring farmers to build dikes and terraces, plant forests and fruit trees, restrain their sheep, and adopt new farming methods. The farmers were also given title to their land to encourage long-term stewardship. Today, hillsides are lush, incomes have gone up, and families who once lived in caves are building homes.

Other government-organized environmental NGOs include the China Environmental Culture Promotion Association (CECPA), which was founded by SEPA in 1992 and restructured by Pan Yue, Vice-Minister of the Ministry of Environmental Protection. Some university think tanks, such as Ma Zhong's Beijing Environment and Development Institute at Renmin University, also occupy a middle ground between a state-run institution with considerable leeway and a truly independent citizens' group. However, the number of GONGOs, although far more numerous than those listed here, is fewer than that of the bottom-up organizations, and the Ministry of Environment Protection and local environmental bureaus have begun to cooperate directly with grassroots ENGOs.

ROLE OF INTERNATIONAL ENGOs

International NGOs have been eager to work in China but have faced numerous difficulties getting permissions and visas and finding Chinese partners, a basic requirement to be able to operate inside the country. One of the best respected of these, China Development Brief, is an informational and networking project for foreign development, charitable, and environmental groups. Founded in 1996, it was shut down in 2007 after more than a decade of dedicated work when the government created visa problems for Nick Young, the English director, whom they accused of conducting unauthorized surveys and forced to leave the country. An all-Chinese version of the organization survives.

The large international conservation NGO the World-Wide Fund for Nature (WWF) was the first international ENGO to have a significant presence in China and has worked in China's Western provinces of Yunnan and Sichuan for decades, adopting the panda as its international logo (Schaller 1993). Conservation International and the Nature Conservancy have more recently established strong programs, with the Nature Conservancy, through its Yunnan Great Rivers project, undertaking to develop and conserve some of China's most beautiful but endangered regions. Conservation International has seen its role primarily as a networker and facilitator, although it also develops conservation models and remains a strong player on the ground, educating consumers in big cities to try to reduce the consumption of wildlife products.

Many other international groups also have active presences in China. The Natural Resources Defense Council is working on climate change, clean energy, environmental governance and green supply chains. Environmental Defense has pioneered carbon trading experiments using market-based approaches to conservation. The World Resources Institute works on population and health as well as transportation. The Sierra Club focuses on energy and trade issues. Pacific Environment focuses on transboundary problems in the Pacific Rim. The International Fund for Animal Welfare, which faces a tremendous task because of China's abominable practices of animal cruelty, is trying to pass animal welfare laws and create a shelter system. One of the early groups to make contact in China was the independent Friends of the Earth/Hong Kong (Hong Kong has been part of China since 1997 but operates under a more democratic political system). Greenpeace, which is widely admired and respected in China, similarly based most of its work from Hong Kong, but its Beijing office and large in-country staff have now grown. The group has taken on such causes as e-waste, genetically modified organisms, and information transparency around air pollution. Such groups generally nurture strong alliances with the Ministry of Environmental Protection as a way of gaining assurance that they will be able to continue their work. While such alliances may limit them, they reflect the Chinese political reality that NGOs need support, whether from the state or from foreign donors. In fact, the voices for environmental protection within the central government are not immune from political threat. By working together, civil society and the parts of the central administration that are trying to shift China onto a more sustainable path strive to strengthen each other and carve out additional political space.

In addition to the big international NGOs with a presence in China, there have been increased efforts by smaller issue-oriented NGOs and domestic groups to link with those in neighboring countries to tackle transboundary issues. International Rivers, based in Berkeley, California, has partnered with small NGOs in the lower reaches of the Salween River in Myanmar and Thailand as well as China to work against the 13 dams planned for the Nu River (as the Salween is called in China), one of China's last pristine free-flowing rivers, whose gorges are nicknamed China's Grand Canyon. Through blogging, public media campaigns, documentary films, and other modes of political engagement (primarily of the symbolic politics type), the group has helped Chinese grassroots groups coalesce around an issue which is both romantic, in that it appeals to young Chinese students' sense of adventure tourism and interest in the exoticism of ethnic minority areas, and hard-hitting, in that it goes to the core of China's energy policy. After fervent public opposition, the Chinese government in 2004 suspended plans for the dams pending further environmental review (Murtha 2008). When the latest five-year plan was announced, it appeared to put the 13 dams proposed for the Nu River back on the table. But soon after, most of the dams were again postponed while seismic and geological studies were being carried out; the Nu River descends through a region heavily laced with fault lines. Farmers and activists recognize that hydropower remains a centerpiece of China's renewable energy portfolio; the Japanese nuclear disaster caused the Chinese to be more cautious in their nuclear plans, especially in earthquake-prone regions, putting renewed pressure on rivers. The massive dam on the Upper Yangzi River at Tiger Leaping Gorge, cancelled after local protests, could yet be revived, or moved upriver into Tibet. The International Rivers Network's website offers additional details (International Rivers Network n.d., b).

ENGO STRATEGIES

There has been a remarkable shift in the strategies and activities of Chinese environmental NGOs, which remain constrained by the need to register with the government and haunted by the threat of closure (Lü and Turner 2006). Understanding the acceptable limits on their activities is a subtle game; permission often rests on political patronage and the degree of freedom available in the country at any given moment, with freedoms contracting during major Party congresses, for example, or during important anniversaries. Often, the demarcation line is not visible until it has been crossed. Nonetheless, ENGOs are expanding their range from traditional programs of environmental education and non-confrontational activities like trash pick-up, tree planting, and advocating for the protection of endangered species like the Tibetan antelope, and are now assuming advocacy roles similar to those adopted by ENGOs in other parts of the world. For example, in 2009 they pressured the government to take greater responsibility for China's role in climate change; more frequently they have served as advocates for communities victimized by pollution. They are exploring tactics of "symbolic politics," as pioneered worldwide by groups like Greenpeace, putting up banners in public places and mounting actions designed to garner media attention. They are taking the lead to pressure the government for greater transparency in disclosing air and water pollution statistics, while taking on powerful corporate interests such as the multinational corporations Monsanto (for genetically modified foods) and Hewlett Packard (for failing to remove toxic components from computers). The adoption of these strategies represents a maturation of Chinese activism and an indication of increased confidence and willingness to take on politically difficult issues. It may also indicate that activists feel safer. The central government's stated commitments to environmental protection provide them with tacit permission, as these official pronouncements open up avenues for "accountability politics." Citizens now have ammunition to hold government agencies to their promises to clean up pollution, improve public safety, and put China on the road to sustainable development.

Internet organization has also become a powerful tool for civil society organizing outside formal group structures, such as when citizens mobilized themselves via cell phone messages to rally against a paraxylene (PX) chemical plant planned by the Xianglu Tenglong

Group in the coastal resort city of Xiamen in Fujian Province in 2007. The following year citizens of Shanghai opposed the building of a magnetic levitation rail line through their neighborhood and organized themselves to "take a walk" on certain days; the phrase is so innocuous and the words in it so common that it cannot be filtered and banned, and participants cannot be arrested because they can claim that they just happened to be in the area. These efforts were successful, although similar efforts by homeowners opposing the extension of a high-speed rail line from Shanghai to Hangzhou managed only to delay the construction until 2010. The 2011 protests against a PX plant in Dalian seem to have met with the most rapid government response so far. Such protests can be understood as a wave of "not in my back yard-ism" (NIMBYism) on the part of a newly empowered Chinese middle class. Unfortunately, in most cases, as elsewhere in the world, NIMBYism often results in the removal of the offending project to a more vulnerable, less well organized community, as we will see in the next chapter.

Another very significant tool for Chinese ENGOs is their alliance with courageous investigative journalists and newspaper editors, who in China have long played a role as advocates for the disenfranchised by speaking truth to power and providing a conduit for information from the grass roots to top leaders who might be in a position to provide justice. Liu Binyan's memoir, *A Higher Kind of Loyalty* (1990) [*Di Er Zhong Zhongcheng* 第二种忠诚] explores this moral obligation in eloquent language. The path-breaking news magazine, *Southern Weekend* [*Nanfang Zhoumo* 南方周末] repeatedly publishes environmental stories at considerable risk to its editors and writers, but despite firings and demotions, the publication's prestige and moral authority have allowed it to remain open. Blogs, the Internet, and instant messaging have also opened up space for the conveyance of environmental information and organizing, as mentioned above.

The international conservation group WildAid has in recent years enlisted the basketball celebrity Yao Ming in its campaign against shark-finning. The use of celebrities to shape and change public opinion and behavior, so common in the West (see Pamela Anderson's work for People for the Ethical Treatment of Animals; Robert Redford, Leonardo DiCaprio, Pierce Brosnan, and Tom Hanks for the Natural Resources Defense Council; and Harrison Ford, the Dixie Chicks, and others for Conservation International), is just beginning in China. It may be a fruitful strategy to increase impact and gain popularity for the environmental cause. As the *New York Times*' Elizabeth Rosenthal reports (2011), "In a commercial made by WildAid, Asian diners at a fancy restaurant begin pushing away their soup bowls as a shark in a nearby tank bleeds from the site where his fin was removed. 'Remember,' says Mr. Yao, the retired basketball player, 'when the buying stops, the killing can, too.'"

Another strategy that Chinese NGOs have recently adopted with enthusiasm is that of survey research, a form of information politics. According to the *China Daily*, the E-waste Civil Action Network conducted a study revealing that 60 percent of Beijing's e-waste is being sold to trash collectors, who pay more than government recycling stations, and that the waste continues to end up in Guangdong Province where cities like Guiyu are hubs of the underground market. The group surveyed 342 residents in downtown Beijing and found that most knew about the dangers of e-waste and placed great hope in NGOs to deal with the problem: "We'll work more actively in the future, as the public expect more from us than from the producers," Lai Yun, director of Greenpeace's pollution control project, told *China Daily*. Lai added that his group is trying to create a mechanism whereby e-waste can be returned to producers for cleaning or disposal. "We hope more international brands will participate in reclaiming their products. This way, they'll be willing to perfect the design of their products to make them easy to be dismantled later" (Wu, Wencong 2011).

Groups have formed domestic and international alliances to conduct extensive investigations into the polluting practices of multinational corporations, such as when Friends of Nature, the Institute of Public and Environmental Affairs, Green Beagle, Envirofriends and Nanjing Green Stone researched Apple Computer's supply chain and exposed serious problems in 27 factories. Over the course of seven months, they interviewed villagers affected by chemical plants that supply Apple components, took water samples that revealed serious pollution levels, and produced an extensive report that they made available electronically (2011), accusing Apple of failing to monitor its supply chain. This exposé came to global attention, and in alliance with United States-based NGOs like the Natural Resources Defense Council, China's Institute for Public and Environmental Affairs led by water activist Ma Jun held discussions in California with Apple executives. Chinese groups have continued to pressure Apple to become more transparent and to take responsibility for its suppliers, forcing Apple to undertake regular talks with environmental groups. This campaign demonstrates increased sophistication in networking and the use of the media to disseminate findings, willingness to take risks by conducting undercover investigations, fearlessness in taking on a powerful multinational corporation whose business is important for China, ability to connect with ordinary villagers who trust such groups to be their voices for justice, and capacity to form transboundary alliances with other members of global civil society to put pressure on a major transnational corporation (Xie 2011).

USE OF THE COURTS

A significant trend in domestic environmental politics is the rise in frequency and scope of environmental litigation and citizens' growing awareness of the courts as a venue to resolve environmental disputes.

Although there are still tremendous weaknesses in the Chinese legal system with regard to implementation and enforcement, and the number of such lawsuits is difficult to quantify, the increase in the use of such tactics is a signal of rising confidence in the rule of law and a growing sense that citizens have right to a clean environment that the state has an obligation to protect. Although the use of the Chinese courts on behalf of pollution victims is far from new, the strategy appears to have achieved broader acceptance, with even ordinary farmers aware of the possibility of bringing their cases to court. This marks a new tool compared with the Chinese culture of dispute resolution. Traditionally, wronged citizens seek to bring a petition to a higher authority by traveling to the front gate of an agency and trying to pass a letter to an influential person inside, or to display a large poster on the sidewalk outside detailing their woes, or to use personal influence or bribery to try to gain redress. The numbers of legal petitioners have grown astronomically as pollution has worsened throughout the country, and more than 40 new specialized courts or tribunals dedicated to hearing environmental lawsuits are now hearing cases, many of them brought by public interest plaintiffs including NGOs, private citizens, and environmental protection bureaus (Wang 2011).

The Center for Legal Assistance to Pollution Victims receives hundreds of appeals for help every month, focusing on aiding the vulnerable in holding polluting factories accountable. The organization has been operating since 1998 at the Chinese University of Political Science and Law and is registered with the Judicial Ministry. Since 1998, advocates have won hundreds of cases and fielded more than 10,000 inquiries, from those of a humble farmer whose ducks were poisoned by chemical pollution to fish farmers whose lawsuit led to the shutdown of a paper-mill in Shandong. Wang Canfa, the founder and director, has gained protection in part by cultivating a high international profile and by housing his Center within a university with close central government ties. He has participated in drafting numerous environmental regulations. The Center has partnered with the Vermont Law School to sponsor environmental law and policy workshops and conferences, including one at National Judges College in Beijing, and their U.S.– China Partnership for Environmental Law recently helped to found China's first environmental public interest law firm (Vermont Law School 2010). Such efforts follow decades of legal exchanges organized by the American Bar Association, the U.S. Department of State's International Visitors' Program, and the National Committee on U.S.– China Relations. However, the focus on environmental law through programs like that of Vermont Law School is comparatively new.

CITIZEN ACTIVISTS

Of course, many ordinary Chinese have motivations for environmental activism thrust upon them, when their villages are contaminated by factories and strange cancer clusters appear, or when a lake that they love or rely upon for fishing becomes toxic. Even fairly uneducated peasant-farmers can become activists in such situations, especially if the pollution or dam gains the attention of an NGO or journalist. One such example is that of the farmer profiled in a remarkable documentary, "Warriors of Qiugang" (Yang 2010). Educated environmental activists provided support to this local leader in his efforts to get a pesticide and dye factory to close down and clean up, but the risk and determination was his alone. Despite the fact that the private owners of the factory had strong ties to local leaders, villagers fought desperately through petitions, lawsuits, and demonstrations, and eventually succeeded in getting the factory to shut. As of the end of the film, however, villagers continued to die of cancer and the clean-up of remaining toxic waste had not been arranged.

This sort of peasant-farmer activism is less likely to succeed than efforts of more educated middle-class citizens, as occurred in the Northern city of Dalian in August 2011 against the Fujia paraxylene

(PX) plant, whose dyke was breached by high ocean waves during a typhoon. As readers will remember, PX is a toxic petrochemical used in the fabric industry to make polyester and other synthetics, and the citizens of Xiamen on the Southern coast fought a similar PX plant, with great success, in 2007. Dalian citizens, learning from their Xiamen neighbors, also used cell texting and "going for a walk" to protest against the plant. According to one news story, "Protesters including children marched holding banners that declared: 'I love Dalian and reject poison,' 'return me my home and garden, get out PX, protect Dalian,' and 'Return my future generations' beautiful home'" (Sui 2011). The authorities, too, seem to have learned from the Xiamen example. The Communist Party chief and the mayor quickly promised to shut and relocate the plant. Protesters were not satisfied without a firm time-table, and their anger broadened against government corruption in general: The plant had been in operation several years before the prerequisite environmental impact assessment was conducted and approved. In the face of organized, educated, urban middle-class mobilization, the government backed down. Greenpeace's Toxics Campaign leader Ma Tianjie told *The Hindu*, "We are seeing more and more cases of middle-class urban residents saying no to polluting projects, and getting involved in such issues ... In urban areas, people are increasingly more aware. With online tools like microblogs, it is also becoming easier to communicate issues to the public" (Krishnan 2011). Indeed, such protests seem to be increasing as the middle class in other cities learns of the success of such protests. Soon after the Dalian incident, protestors in a city near Shanghai demonstrated against a chronically polluting solar panel production plant, while in December 2011, in the fishing village of Haimen in Guangdong province, protesters blocked an expressway in opposition to a planned coal-fired power plant, claiming that existing plants had caused cancer and a drop in fishing yields. This protest ended in violent confrontations with riot police and a suspension of the project. Protests over similar issues are sure to follow.

Calls for government transparency and accountability are thus increasingly accompanying thousands of "environmental mass incidents" whose numbers increase every year. That the government reports numbers of such incidents in the official press is encouraging, perhaps indicating increased confidence in addressing public outrage. This is further backed up by research that suggests overall mass incidents in China have risen from an official total of 9,000 a year in 1994 to an estimated 127,000 in 2008 (Wedeman 2009).

There are many other cases of local citizens trying to hold polluting enterprises accountable, but their stories are largely left untold to the outside world. Consider the parents of children with lead poisoning and the residents of Panyu, Guangdong Province, whose citizen lawsuit eventually forced the Dongtai tannery to pay compensation after numerous discharges of contaminated wastewater. Also largely unknown to the international community is the story of the Huai River Defenders, led by local resident Huo Daishan, who was motivated to do something about the extensive chemical effluents in the river when his childhood friend died of cancer. In Hunan province's Xiangtan city, an ordinary citizen's online "green appeal" campaign to clean up Yujia Lake successfully pressured officials to promise to reverse pollution trends.

Often such activism is met with threats and political repression, for these "ordinary people" do not usually have the backing of international ties and or sophistication in navigating the political system, unlike highly educated urban activists, and they are fighting powerful developers, factory owners, and political interests. Many farmers faced with dislocation for dams simply acknowledge their own powerlessness in the face of the state. They know the risks in resisting and believe it to be dangerous, if not futile. They see the examples of Lake Tai activist Wu Lihong who, after tirelessly fighting to clean one of China's largest and most polluted bodies of water, was sentenced in 2007 on a trumped-up charge of extortion and blackmail. Zhejiang activist and founder of "Green Watch" Tan Kai was arrested for illegally obtaining "state secrets" in 2005 and denied legal representation. He served a full 18-month sentence. An activist working to clean up Dianchi Lake in Yunnan Province was similarly threatened and beaten. And farmers resisting forcible relocations for the Three Gorges Dam have been arrested and prosecuted. Meanwhile, as mentioned, nature reserve officers have died fighting poachers, like the Tibetan brothers-in-law who died defending the Tibetan antelope.

Such tales illustrate the connection between environmental protection and political repression in developing countries. In developed countries, activists often work in different spheres than do those concerned with human rights. However, in the developing world, this sharp distinction often does not exist, for two main reasons: First, the political rights of environmental activists to free speech and assembly, due process, and freedom from torture are often violated, so environmentalists become human rights victims. Second, in the developing world, with its intense pollution problems, the right to clean air and water is clearly identified with the right to life, the most fundamental of all the human rights. At the global level, an effort to articulate these connections has been ongoing in the form of the Earth Charter Initiative, where a multinational team of activists and civil society groups has drafted a document that expresses the connections among ecological protection, justice, peace, democracy, and human rights. Although activists hope that it will someday formally be signed at the United Nations much like the human rights covenants, to date the initiative has flourished primarily at the grass roots. The charter has been endorsed primarily by civil society groups, although international organizations such as the United Nations Educational, Scientific and Cultural Organization (UNESCO) and the International Union for Conservation of Nature (IUCN) have also supported it. The Initiative's official mission is "to promote the transition to sustainable ways of living and a global society founded on a shared ethical framework that includes respect and care for the community of life, ecological integrity, universal human rights, respect for diversity, economic justice, democracy, and a culture of peace." By articulating values in this way, the Earth Charter Initiative shows how civil society can participate in global governance without formal governmental approval or power.

QUESTIONS FOR RESEARCH AND DISCUSSION

1 Can you identify some of the creative ways that Chinese advocacy groups have attempted to achieve their goals? Can you suggest additional strategies they might employ? What are the strengths and limitations of Internet-based activism?

2 How does the situation of Chinese activists shed light on the relationship between environmental protection and human rights? Compare the Universal Declaration of Human Rights with the Earth Charter (both easily available online). Which would be easier to implement and enforce in China and in your own country? Where are the areas of overlap and divergence?

3 What is the role of China's middle class in environmental change? Is its newfound wealth a positive or negative force, or both? What is the connection between the rise of the middle class and civil society?

4 What do you think about the role of GONGOs in China? Are they an effective way for the government to mobilize people while exerting a measure of social control? Do different advocacy groups have different approaches to try to create social change? Where are the leverage points for social change in your community?

ADDITIONAL RESOURCES

- "In China, Human Costs Are Built Into an iPad," an exposé of Apple's supply chain by Charles Duhigg and David Barboza. Available on *The New York Times* website.
- "Rainmakers," a documentary by Floris-Jan Van Luyn. Information available at: http://www.imdb.com/title/tt1688074/
- "Shielding the Mountains," a documentary by Emily Yeh. Information available at: http://www.tibetsacredmountain.org
- "Shifting Nature," part three of the PBS documentary "China from the Inside" by Jonathan Lewis. Information and trailer available at: http://www.pbs.org/kqed/chinainside/nature/index.html
- "Silent Nu River," a documentary by Hu Jie. Information and trailer available at: http://www.visiblerecord.com/en/films/?id=C010
- "Waking the Green Tiger," a documentary by Gary Marcuse. Information and trailer available at: www.facetofacemedia.ca/page.php?sectionID=2
- "Warriors of Qiugang," 39-minute documentary by Ruby Yang and Thomas Lennon. Full film available at: http://e360.yale.edu/feature/the_warriors_of_qiugang_a_chinese_village_fights_back/2358/
- U.S. Embassy-Beijing, list of Chinese environmental NGOs at: http://beijing.usembassy-china.org.cn/esth_engo.html
- Wolfgang Sachs, Environment and Human Rights, Wuppertal Paper No. 137 (September 2003), Wuppertal Institute for Climate, Environment, and Energy. Available at: http://www.uibk.ac.at/peacestudies/downloads/peacelibrary/environment.pdf

6 Environmental Justice and the Displacement of Environmental Harm

The inseparable links between environmental sustainability and social justice are increasingly well recognized. Without social justice, the extraction of resources all too often simply displaces harm across time and space, postponing our confrontation with the limits of the planet's bounty and concealing the costs of our consumption. Some would even extend the concern for justice across species, as humans encroach on the habitat of other living creatures and drive them to extinction, tearing apart the web of life on which we ultimately depend. This chapter focuses on achieving justice across geographic space in the human world. First, however, let us reflect on the temporal dimensions of this problem.

Great attention has been paid to the fact that the world is reaching the limits to resources – indeed, our basic understanding of sustainability rests on the effort to achieve equity between those now alive and those not yet born, or justice for future generations. Unfortunately, traditional economic systems, from Marxism to capitalism, have failed to account for the depletion of natural capital and have often measured environmental degradation or resources consumption as simply another form of economic activity contributing to growth. The inadequacy of these theories is clearly demonstrated in our study of the environmental crisis in China: Aggressive development without internalization of real environmental costs, left unchecked, could undermine many of China's gains. Minerals, fossil fuels, timber, and agricultural resources are already growing scarce even as China's heavy pollution, increasingly inflicted on the poor and vulnerable, damages health and leads to social unrest that threatens the government's credibility, authority, and legitimacy.

Increasingly, the world's policy makers are paying attention not only to the temporal dimensions of displacement of harm but also to the spatial ones. For those who are sensitive to the dynamic of displacement, sustainability will never be achieved without distributive justice among those currently alive. *Inter-generational equity*, which considers the rights of future generations to the same "natural capital" available to people alive today, cannot be separated from the politically contentious *intra-generational equity*, which considers the rights of all people to have fair access to and benefits from the world's resources. The United Nations Development Program (UNDP)'s 2011 annual report, *Sustainability and Equity: A Better Future for All* elaborates on the links between environmental degradation and injustice: "A joint lens shows how environmental degradation intensifies inequality through adverse impacts on already disadvantaged people and how inequalities in human development amplify environmental degradation … Inequalities are especially unjust when they systematically disadvantage specific groups of people, whether because of gender, race or birthplace, or when the gap is so great that acute poverty is high" (Klugman 2011). In another indication of the wide acceptance of these links, the United Nations environmental conferences, Stockholm (1972), Rio (1992), and Johannesburg (2002), affirmed that sustainability rests on three pillars, the environmental, the economic, and the social, while the Earth Summit in Rio de Janeiro (2012) focused on creating an institutional framework for sustainable development in the context of poverty eradication. The Earth Charter, mentioned in the previous chapter, also plumbs these interconnections.

Environmental injustice across space occurs at many different levels and scales. It can occur within large cities among neighborhoods;

between urban and rural areas; between wealthy and less wealthy regions within a single country; and across borders, between countries forced by economic necessity to receive environmental harms and those who can afford to export them. We have already noted the extreme wealth gap between residents of Chinese cities and the countryside and seen how poor communities, less well-organized and politically powerful than their neighbors, often bear the brunt when a well-organized urban middle class forces a polluting factory to relocate. This chapter explores these ideas in greater detail. We home in on several examples. First we look at the problems of where to site landfills, at the unhealthy living conditions of the millions of rural migrants who make up the "floating populations" in the slums outside some of China's major cities, and at rural "cancer villages." The bulk of the chapter then explores regional inequalities between the wealthy coastal areas in the East and the less developed Western border regions where so many ethnic minority nationalities live, because tensions in places like Tibet and Inner Mongolia are fraught with implications for China's future as a unified state capable of delivering justice and a good livelihood to all of its citizens. We finally turn to international examples. In some cases, China is an importer and victim of environmental injustice, as in Southern Guangzhou, a center for the international electronic waste recycling business. However, China is also an exporter and source of environmental injustice, as the newly wealthy country displaces environmental harms onto less developed countries, extracting resources from Ecuador to Nigeria and often creating pollution and environmental degradation in the process. Although the latter topic is largely beyond the scope of a volume that focuses on domestic problems, it is much in the news these days as countries try to understand how China's rise will affect them, on the one hand welcoming Chinese aid and investment, and on the other wary about becoming dependent upon a new superpower whose role in the international system is still being defined.

We must start with a few definitions of the inter-related concepts of environmental justice and environmental injustice. The Central European University Center for Environmental Policy and Law (2007) provides these useful articulations:

A condition of environmental justice exists when environmental risks and hazards and investments and benefits are equally distributed with a lack of discrimination, whether direct or indirect, at any jurisdictional level; and when access to environmental investments, benefits, and natural resources are equally distributed; and when access to information, participation in decision making, and access to justice in environment-related matters are enjoyed by all.

By contrast,

An environmental injustice exists when members of disadvantaged, ethnic, minority or other groups suffer disproportionately at the local, regional (sub-national), or national levels from environmental risks or hazards, and/or suffer disproportionately from violations of fundamental human rights as a result of environmental factors, and/or denied access to environmental investments, benefits, and/or natural resources, and/or are denied access to information; and/or participation in decision making; and/or access to justice in environment-related matters.

We note in these definitions the important themes of information access and transparency, public participation, fairness, and equity; we also see that environmental injustice issues can be expressed both as "brown" (pollution) problems or "green" (resource extraction) problems. Environmental injustice thus occurs locally, regionally, and nationally; it also occurs internationally in a globalized world, as strong countries protect their own territories from degradation while pushing it onto more vulnerable ones. This is conceptually distinct from one country controlling and consuming another's natural resources with impunity because of power imbalances, as the West did in the great era of colonialism, although that dynamic remains in play.

It should be noted that this line of inquiry does not grapple with the much thornier question of whether the world's human population can ever achieve environmental justice on a global scale, given our exploding numbers and tremendous rate of consumption of the world's limited resources. Government and community leaders naturally seek to safeguard the best interests of the populations over which they have jurisdiction or which they seek to represent, so it is not surprising that they resist pollution and environmental degradation or choose to locate it where there is least political resistance. Poor communities may feel they have little choice about hosting such activities, or decide that the benefits in terms of jobs and revenue outweigh the costs in scarred landscapes, disease, and shortened life spans. As we human beings search the globe for ever-scarcer materials to sustain our consumption and run out of places to dispose of the solid and toxic waste that we produce, the effort to achieve environmental justice starts to feel like aiming at a moving target: A problem pops up in a new location as soon as one has been resolved.

We must thus recognize the difficulty in achieving distributive justice. As long as our society relies on landfills, coal-fired power plants, and animal feedlots, they will have to go somewhere, creating inequity that fuels tensions. The "Not in My Backyard" (NIMBY) phenomenon underscores the importance of the word "displacement." One country's clean-up often means another's toxic sludge, garbage incinerator, or nuclear waste repository; one community's victory spells another's bad news. "Locally undesirable land uses," or LULUs, are worldwide phenomena, unwelcome externalities of modern industrialization. As we begin this discussion of environmental justice as it relates to China, then, we should remind ourselves that these dynamics occur almost everywhere. What Chinese neighborhoods, municipalities, and the state itself are doing to resist and shift extractive industries and manu-facturing plants is little different from what others have been doing for centuries. Moreover, middle-class urban Han Chinese, like elites throughout the world, tend to believe themselves to be superior to rural farmers, ethnic minorities, and the poor, whether consciously or uncon-sciously, and see themselves as deserving of higher standards of envi-ronmental quality. Racism and classism are worldwide problems. The main differences in the case of China are those of scale, impact, and rapidity, and of the Chinese state's willingness to be heavy-handed, sometimes even brutal, in the achievement of its goals.

ENVIRONMENTAL JUSTICE IN THE URBAN SETTING

Cities around the world struggle with where to dispose of household waste. New in China is the NIMBY-ism of the middle class, which is often heralded as a form of environmental awakening and emerging civil society, while less attention is given to where the harm goes when a community successfully resists. As the Chinese middle class finds its political voice and demands a better environment, the clean-up of urban cores often causes areas near or just outside city boundaries to receive greater amounts of pollution. One of the most highly contested environmental problems in China is disposal of garbage. Landfills are expected to fill completely within a few years and are the sources of noise and stench, large amounts of methane (a highly destructive greenhouse gas), and toxics that leach into local groundwater, while incinerators can disperse toxics into the air where they spread even more widely.

As the New York Times' Keith Bradsher wrote in 2009 in his story "China's incinerators loom as a global hazard," China has already sur-passed the U.S. in overall production of household garbage. Provincial and local governments are now building incinerators as partial solutions to overflowing garbage dumps, but many of these are associated with the production of toxic emissions of dioxin, mercury, and cadmium, which affect local residents but also float into the atmosphere and can be measured around the world. Residents of the wealthy cities of Shanghai and Beijing have demanded high levels of pollution control, and some of those incinerators are up to international standards. Yet in the poorer interior of the country, dioxin emissions are permitted to be ten times higher than those in the European Union and mercury levels are dangerously high. If China does not soon take steps to limit these emissions, global dioxin levels could double.

Even in wealthier cities, unease about the use of incinerators is growing, not least in the capital city of Beijing, which as of 2009 was producing nearly 20,000 tons of garbage a day and was set to exceed capacity in all 23 of its waste treatment plants within a few years. Planned incinerators have been met with widespread protests. For example, in 2009 residents of the university area in Northwest Beijing's Haidian District mobilized to oppose plans to build an incinerator at the unpopular and nearly full Liulitun landfill, already the source of much unpleasant stench and noise. Residents argued that an incinerator would produce dioxin, mercury, and other toxics, and were heartened when the Ministry of Environmental Protection spoke out against the idea and in favor of improved recycling. After citizens launched protests stretching over many months and brought a lawsuit that succeeded in raising pressure and publicity, the government abandoned plans for an incinerator at that location. Local officials connected to the landfill were imprisoned for corruption, and one even committed suicide while in detention. However, even as Liulitun fills to capacity, a replacement incinerator is planned for Dagong village on the Western border of the city, near several scenic districts, where 2,000 tons of garbage per day will be burned to reduce volume and generate electricity. The government claims that fewer people will be impacted at the new location and that there will be information available about the pollutants produced (China Radio International 2011). But what is most clear about this shift of location is that the farmers of Dagong do not have the political clout to resist this "locally undesirable land use."

Other victims of urban environmental injustice can also be found near city boundaries: They are the marginalized rural migrants who make up China's "floating population." Urbanization and the relaxation of the residence card system have created conditions for the mobility of millions of farmers who travel to cities in search of employment, most of which is temporary work in factories and construction sites or as nannies and housemaids. Because their status is semi-legal in that they do not have rights to health care, schooling, or other government services, and they have limited funds, they often live in temporary shelters in city outskirts or in makeshift dormitories near construction sites. Sanitation conditions are poor and access to health care restricted. Lacking sewage treatment plants, waste from their communities spills directly into waterways and is a source of serious pollution. These marginalized migrants often suffer environmental contamination from indoor coal-burning for heat and fuel, unclean water for drinking and washing, and overcrowded and uncomfortable living situations that promote the spread of disease. Now that waste transfer stations and incinerators are increasingly sited on city outskirts, the migrant poor also bear the brunt of the toxic pollution, noise, and unsanitary conditions from these. While China's urban slums are nowhere near the scale of those of some cities in India or Brazil, this is in part because the government periodically rounds up the migrants, demolishes their homes and makeshift schools, and attempts to make them return whence they came. However, there are few paid jobs back home, and life from farming remains at a subsistence level, so these migrants continue to eke out a hard existence as a marginalized underclass that supports China's growth and the lifestyles of the urban middle class. This mimics the rural-to-urban migration patterns of much of the developing world, but China's migration restrictions complicate legal and human rights matters even as they purport to combat an avalanche of slums.

As cities attempt to clean up their urban cores not only by relocating landfills but also by shutting and shifting polluting factories such as the PX factories that residents of Xiamen and Dalian fought so successfully, these manufacturing facilities are often moved to peri-urban areas where members of the floating population can pick up poorly paid work and local entrepreneurs and officials can continue to earn profits, often while flouting environmental regulations. As Xuemei Bai (2008) writes, "Many cities are relocating their most polluting industries outside their boundaries. Although these cities are subsequently praised by the central Government for their improved inner-city environmental quality, often the only real change is that the offending industries and their associated pollution are simply moved to neighboring cities or to surrounding rural areas." That was the case during the lead-up to the 2008 Olympics, which saw the government strenuously clean up the air in order to deliver on its promises to the International Olympic Committee.

ENVIRONMENTAL JUSTICE AT THE URBAN-RURAL DIVIDE: CANCER VILLAGES AND OTHER DISEASE CLUSTERS

We have mentioned the horrific phenomenon of cancer villages in previous chapters. These are rural communities located near highly polluting chemical factories. Cancer and other diseases are so highly concentrated that entire families are known to grow sick and die. A Chinese investigative journalist has posted an online map (listed under Additional Resources at the end of this chapter) which shows the locations of more than 100 of these, but many suspect that the real figure is many times higher. While these cancer villages tend to be concentrated near wealthy cities in China's East, where international businesses have invested in joint ventures and manufacturing plants to take advantage of cheap labor and lax environmental laws, such villages may increasingly be emerging in the less developed West, where jobs are scarce and information about pollution difficult to obtain. In Northeast Yunnan's Xinglong, for example, where an industrial park's paper mills and chemical factories discharge effluent into the river and fumes into the air, residents told the *Guardian's* Jonathan Watts (2010a), "Before the factories were built, there was no cancer…Now we hear every year that this person or that person has cancer, especially lung and liver cancer." A tenth of the village's goats died.

Cancer villages in the wealthy East tend to be in poor counties near major cities and at the deltas of the Yellow, Yangzi, and Pearl Rivers, while inland they are clustered near rivers. Geographer Lee Liu's systematic study of cancer villages (2010) identifies media and internet reports on 459 cancer villages, with every province except Tibet and Qinghai containing at least a few; sources include the prestigious China Central Television. The cancer clusters are most intense in poor farming villages where highly polluting industries are located. Liu writes,

> There seems to be a spatial pattern of environmental injustice in the cancer-village belt, for the location of cancer villages within and between provinces….China has made major efforts in environmental protection in the past decades, including the establishment of eco-communities and model environmental cities; however, the cancer villages prove that China's efforts are only partially successful….The rich, some of whom got rich through the polluting factories, live in better environmental conditions, while poor farmers live by the factories and suffer from the pollution on a daily basis.

The notorious Huai River basin has produced some of the worst cases: In the whole of China, the county of Shenqiu in Northwest

Henan has the most cancer villages, one of which, Huangmengying, a village of only 2,400 people, saw 118 die in the decade between 1994 and 2004, half of them of cancer; 80 percent of young people are constantly ill. In some of these villages, the death rate is higher than the birth rate, and villagers are heavily in debt because of medical bills (the documentary "Warriors of Qiugang," mentioned in Chapter Five, portrays a cancer village in the Huai River basin, in Anhui Province).

Other rural environmental justice problems occur in villages near battery smelters where widespread lead poisoning has left almost all of the local children with cognitive and developmental problems. Similar problems are caused by cadmium and mercury contamination stemming from poorly managed recycling of electronic waste shipped to China from Europe and North America, as discussed more fully later in this chapter. The impact of these toxic wastes has, Human Rights Watch alleges (2011), been covered up and tests have been falsified by the government.

What identifies these problems as issues of environmental justice is that the residents of these villages are largely poor and sometimes illiterate, with limited ability to organize politically, use the legal system, or seek redress. As we saw in the last chapter, among the heroic groups that have stepped in to help these people seek justice, despite harassment and even arrests, are Wang Canfa's Center for Legal Assistance to Victims of Pollution, Green Anhui, Huo Daishan's group the Huai River Defenders, and the Chongqing Green Volunteers Alliance. Ma Jun's Institute for Public and Environmental Affairs is developing an online water pollution database to pressure companies to clean up and provide information to activists and villagers; we have also seen how Greenpeace's undercover efforts to track effluents from shoe manufacturers have caused these international businesses to promise to change their ways. As in the case of the air pollution mentioned earlier for Beijing, such information transparency is a critical weapon in the pursuit of environmental equity. The Ministry of Environmental

Protection's efforts to make pollution reports public, especially since the issuance of the 2008 Measures for the Disclosure of Environmental Information, have supported these campaigns.

ENVIRONMENTAL JUSTICE BETWEEN CHINA'S EAST AND WEST

Some of the most poignant Chinese examples of environmental injustice can be found between the developed coastal areas and the peripheral, largely minority-occupied regions of the borders which are rich in natural resources such as fossil fuels, minerals, timber, and rivers that can be dammed to produce hydroelectric power. This complicated dynamic requires us to reflect on the nature of the state itself, and then to plumb specific examples of these vast but comparatively less populated border areas.

One of the state's primary functions is the extraction of resources, with degradation as a common by-product. This phenomenon is far from new. For centuries the less developed Western and frontier areas of China have seen the state try to secure resource-rich territory for exploitation for use by the developed coastal areas. Stevan Harrell (1997) has described how such efforts have been framed in a discourse of "civilizing," "liberating," "developing," and "modernizing" a "backwards" people for their own good. In recognition of problems in its handling of Han-minority relations and out of concern for the increasing wealth gap between China's rich and poor, in 1999 the state launched a "Develop the West" or "Open up the West" campaign [*xibu da kaifa* 西部大开发]. The program is officially intended to decrease severe economic inequalities between the coastal areas and the hinterlands. Critics argue that this campaign may also be motivated by a wish to maintain social stability. As the core in the East grows wealthy, those on the periphery are left behind and they grow increasingly resentful, posing challenges to Beijing's authority. Whatever the underlying motivation, critics say, this campaign, with its focus on infrastructure investments such as roads, railroads, dams, and power plants, primarily facilitates resource extraction that benefits coastal areas and produces only nominal benefits for local populations.

The spatial displacement of environmental harm to contested "autonomous" regions on China's periphery such as Xinjiang, Inner Mongolia, Tibet, Qinghai, and Ningxia, and to provinces like Gansu and Yunnan shares common patterns. Resources are exploited in places where local ethnic minority people who have nominal power to govern themselves tend to be excluded from the benefits of such exploitation. While some of these provinces are officially "autonomous," they have little self-governing power; Jonathan Watts describes them ironically as places where people are "free to do anything Beijing likes" (2010b, p. 208). Historically, state-organized activities have led to an increase in such environmental problems as deforestation, erosion, inappropriate land use, desertification, nuclear waste, and increased population pressures on local ecosystems. In these regions, political repression and extractive activities have been closely linked (Shapiro 2001).

The situation in these regions reminds us of one of our core questions: Can China deal with the acute poverty in much of the country, even as parts of the nation grow rich? Or do poverty-alleviation programs end up masking and contributing to a dynamic of environmental and political exploitation, sometimes even despite the best of intentions of policy makers? While the various ethnic minority border regions have their own histories due to vastly different geographies and cultural traditions, we will focus on just two well-known examples: Inner Mongolia and Tibet.

Inner Mongolia

The Inner Mongolian Autonomous Region (to be distinguished from Mongolia, an independent country) was a target for post-Liberation "settling the border" campaigns. Han Chinese were encouraged to move to the frontiers in multiple waves to civilize restive ethnic minority nationalities such as the Mongols, whose nomadic lifestyles were considered backwards. This state-building effort to relocate Han to the borders culminated during the Cultural Revolution with a campaign to mobilize against the Soviet Union and also to grow cereals in a "grain first" effort to "Prepare against war, Prepare against famine, Serve the people." The campaign reflected China's deep insecurity about food supply during the years immediately following the 1959–1961 state-induced famine (Becker 1997; Dikötter 2010). This effort to convert grasslands into farmland during the 1970s, chronicled in Ma Bo's memoir, translated into English as *Blood Red Sunset* (1996), was ultimately abandoned after the ecological damage became apparent and many Han were permitted to return home to the cities. At that point, the emphasis shifted to herding, with additional disastrous consequences from overgrazing, leading the state to shift to promote farming, livestock pens, and mining.

Nowadays, traditionally nomadic Mongol herders are being moved to urban centers as part of an "ecological migration" policy adopted in 2001. The government argues that nomadism and overgrazing are responsible for the degradation of the grasslands and the expansion of the desert, which now lies only four hours from the capital. The sandstorms that sweep Beijing and drift as far away as Japan and Korea, and even to the U.S. and Canadian West Coasts, often originate here. In truth, the government may be more interested in securing access to grasslands to expand mining, commercial ranching and farming to satisfy the appetites of China's newly wealthy, and therefore is using "ecological migration" as a convenient excuse to eradicate traditional ethnic ways of living that may challenge Han authority. As scholar James Scott has pointed out in his important book, *Seeing like a State* (1998), the ideology of modernization often leads states to use authoritarian means to reconfigure populations for state-building purposes.

The environmental damage that the state attributes to the nomads has also in large part been created by past policies of the central government. When concern for the environment (and for minority cultures) is low on the list of state priorities, enormous damage and disruption can be inflicted in a relatively short period of time. In the late 1950s, herders were pushed into "People's Communes," large-scale economic and social institutions designed to speed up China's social and political transformation toward socialism. Then, in the rush to dismantle the communes in the post-Mao era, the land and herds were split up and assigned and contracted to individual families. The government failed to recognize that grazing requires flexibility to adjust and adapt to climatic variability, and that combining herds may be highly efficient, since only a small number of shepherds are required to monitor a herd. Local people resisted attempts to replace goats and sheep with penned cattle, for indigenous Mongols regard the nomadic lifestyle as an integral part of their cultural identity, as described so powerfully in Jiang Rong's *Wolf Totem* (2008).

Government officials ignored indigenous knowledge and traditional practices which had helped to maintain an ecological balance in the past. Local herders could have told them that wolves play a key role in preserving the ecological balance of the grasslands, and that corralled animals that can smell fresh grass will not eat hay and thus starve at the very moment that their strength is needed most for lambing. Similarly, when the government attempted to restore sections of the grassland, officials ignored the need for livestock paths to get at water and forage. As a result, poor and disenfranchised villagers have ended up employing what James Scott (1985) calls "weapons of the weak" to dodge enforcement, grazing their animals at night to avoid detection, hiding animal numbers by cooperating with one another to exceed per-household quotas, and paying off local officials (Wang, Xiaoyi 2007). Yet the state insists that it knows what is best for the local people even as they protest that their very identities are under assault.

Environmental protection is being used as a banner to bring frontier populations into eco-modernity even though sought-for environmental improvements are widely acknowledged as unattained (Yeh 2009).

Meanwhile, intensive mining has become a source of tension between indigenous Mongols and the mining companies that have flooded to take advantage of the intensified demand for coal and the "rare earths" elements of which China controls a near-monopoly, used in electronics, solar panels, and high-tech defense equipment. Inner Mongolia now supplies one quarter of China's massive consumption of coal, in part because reserves lie near the surface and are relatively easy to extract, a powerful draw in a country where the underground mining industry is the most dangerous in the world. Conflicts with herders have resulted. In May 2011, two Mongol herdsmen who were trying to keep their traditional grazing grounds from being polluted and destroyed were killed, one of them run over by a truck and another killed during a protest over pollution. Their deaths sparked further protests and short-term government imposition of martial law. Dru Gladney, an anthropologist who studies Chinese minorities, told the *Los Angeles Times*' David Pierson that such conflicts between coal and grassland "are tinderbox issues for the Mongols. They do not think they are always benefiting from the resources being extracted" (2011). As more traditional grazing land is fenced off for mines, such conflicts can be expected to worsen.

In Inner Mongolia, the state initially distorted sustainable human–nature balances and traditional grassland use by promoting in-migration and land transformation in order to grow grain, and then justified heavy-handed interference with local culture through the use of an environmental protection discourse. In the name of "ecological resettlement," nomads are prevented from allowing their animals to roam freely and forced to move into towns and cities where the state can control them more easily, even as mining companies move in to exploit the rich reserves beneath the grasslands. The use of the grasslands as a sustainable resource is essentially a thing of the past, since desertification is one of the most difficult forms of environmental degradation to reverse; the state's heavy investment in "Green Belt" afforestation and reforestation projects, which began shortly after the 1949 revolution and has intensified in recent years as desertification inches toward Beijing, has had only mixed results over the decades. At the present moment, the state has combined its disparate goals of ecological protection and assertion of Han-style national identity. Using environmental protection as a pretext for suppression of ethnic identities perceived to threaten national unity, the state has forced herders to get out of the way of the mining companies, some of which are large multinational investors. In terms of environmental injustice, ethnic minorities whose very identities are tied up in traditional uses of the landscape have suffered grievously as a result of degradation and overuse from which they have received little benefit.

Tibet

Greater Tibet (which includes the Tibetan Autonomous Region and parts of Gansu, Sichuan, Qinghai, and Yunnan) provides another poignant example of China's problems with dramatic environmental injustice in border regions. As in other frontier areas, the state plays a leading role in resource extraction and environmental degradation – and concomitant repression of local cultures and national identities. Extreme as the damage already is, the greatest destruction likely lies in the future. The railroad between low-lying Golmud in Qinghai Province and the Tibetan capital of Lhasa was completed only in 2006, and more railroads are in the planning stages. Despite the fanfare about the development benefits that the railroad will bring to Tibet, it is also expected to bring an increase in extraction of precious metals and minerals and an influx of Han migrants, who will outnumber local Tibetans in the foreseeable future. Multiple new airports will further facilitate Han control of the region and consolidate military power along the contested border with India. Such infrastructure development will effectively render impotent Tibetan efforts to contest Chinese claims of sovereignty.

China's treatment of Tibet illustrates how history, politics, state security, and a lack of respect for indigenous cultures can combine with devastating impact on the environment. China's claim to Tibet is based on a brief period in the distant past, during the Tang dynasty (618–907), when Chinese princess Wen Cheng was married to Tibetan king Songtsen Gampo. Following the 1949 revolution and the founding of the People's Republic, China "liberated" Tibet from the rule of the Dalai Lama, claiming a role as liberator of a feudal society in which corrupt monks extracted wealth from a backwards people. An attempted uprising in 1959 was forcibly suppressed, and the Dalai Lama escaped into exile in Northern India. This story and these competing claims to Tibet are well told in a book by John Avedon, *In Exile from the Land of Snows* (1984) and in the Dalai Lama's own memoir, *Freedom in Exile* (1990).

The impact of China's exploitation of Tibetan resources will be felt throughout Asia. Many of the great rivers of Asia rise in the Tibetan Plateau, including the Indus, Brahmaputra, Yangzi, Yellow, Salween (Nu), and Mekong. Dams and global warming will affect the Himalayan ice fields that feed the rivers, which will have an impact on China as well as surrounding countries. Industrial pollution of the headwaters could prove disruptive well beyond the "roof of the world." Such degradation will be tragic given the traditional Tibetan commitment to sustainability, with cultural and religious beliefs forbidding the unnecessary killing of animals, pollution of water, disruption of soil, and excessive logging (Lowe 1992).

Much environmental degradation in Greater Tibet has already occurred. Many old-growth forests were cut during the decades after the Communist victory in 1949. Although logging in western China was banned in 1998 after the government recognized that widespread soil erosion was contributing to heavy flooding downstream, illegal deforestation continues. Grasslands have already been severely degraded both in the Tibetan Autonomous Region itself and in traditionally Tibetan areas in Gansu, Qinghai, and Sichuan. In 2009, state-media agency *Xinhua* reported Chinese officials as acknowledging desertification in Tibet proper to be spreading by almost 100,000 *mu* (one mu = about 0.16 acres) a year. Some scholars believe this degradation is essentially desertification wrought by climate change, although not all agree (Gao et al. 2006; Harris 2010).

Until the completion of the railroad connecting Xining and Lhasa, China's determination to conquer and hold Tibet could best be explained by the state's perceived need for a buffer between China and India, with which it has had hostile relations for decades; the lengthy disputed border between China and India remains politically unresolved in part because of Chinese difficulty with supply lines. The railroad will allow China to confront India with much greater ease and may change the power equation. The railroad does not merely alter the geo-strategic political calculus, however. It can also be seen as a way of drawing Tibet and its rich mineral and water resources into the bosom of China proper, permitting industry to locate there for the first time. While Tibetans traditionally do not mine because they believe that to do so takes from the earth's strength, the Chinese are eager to exploit the 126 identified minerals to be found there, which include uranium, lithium, chromite, boron, borax, iron, gold, copper, silver, and zinc, as well as oil and gas. Moreover, China plans to build more than 750 dams, including one near the ethnic Tibetan city of Deqen in Yunnan, on the Upper Yangzi, which would replace a massive dam planned for Tiger Leaping Gorge that was canceled after intense efforts by local farmers and Beijing activists. In Tibet proper, a hydropower station site at Yamdrok Yumtso, a large holy lake which is believed to contain the spirit of Tibet, is guarded by 1,500 Chinese People's

Liberation Army troops; the planned dam will provide electricity for Lhasa, which has increasingly become a Han city being used as an overflow valve for excess population from the East (Moore 2008). Finally, China's plans for Greater Tibet include the planned Western route for the South-North Water Transfer, a highly controversial and technically difficult engineering feat which, if accomplished, would have major ecological impacts on the Tibetan plateau as well as Southwestern rivers like the Mekong and Salween that drain into Southeast Asia. The "land of snows" that once seemed so alien and forbidding, whence Han were sent only for hardship posts, has now become so Sinicized that Han are beginning to find it an attractive relocation option.

Tibet, along with other Western ethnic minority regions like Yunnan, has also been heavily influenced by millions of Han Chinese tourists, who once could not dream of traveling for vacation. Now, with disposable income for the first time, they are on the move. Such regions have captured the popular imagination as romantic destinations for ecotourism and ethnotourism. As elsewhere in minority regions, with the profit motive dominant, tourists are "consuming" both people and nature. Entrepreneurs from as far away as Shenzhen near Hong Kong are buying up ethnic products, shops, and small inns in minority regions, so much that this has affected local artists' choices about what to produce and profoundly distorted local culture. Tour groups are taken to minority villages where local people dressed in traditional costume perform welcome ceremonies and offer music, dance, traditional crafts, and lunch. The commodification of culture also extends to the great monasteries of Tibet that were once the crown jewels of Tibetan history and culture, in the style of universities. Now these places of worship and study are under tight military control and all but emptied of the tens of thousands of monks who once learned and practiced Tibetan Buddhism there. Tourist groups often interrupt the sacred rituals and devotional practices of those who remain, and there is great political tension between monks and authorities. To accommodate more tourists, authorities have suggested building a "mini Potala" on a nearby hill. Meanwhile, in traditionally Tibetan areas in Western Sichuan and Northern Yunnan, national parks such as Napahai and Jiuzhaigou are being transformed into profit centers. Rather than continuing to permit a fluid boundary system in which local people can sustainably use and profit from the reserves, officials are experimenting with a Western-style system of "fortress conservation" with impermeable boundaries, high ticket prices, and tourist access through government controlled buses. Local people who once generated income by providing local lodging and horse rides are being excluded. In some cases, they are even forced to move outside park boundaries and forbidden from pursuing traditional light subsistence activities.

The Voice of America reported that on July 19, 2011, speaking in Lhasa in front of the Potala Palace at a ceremony marking the 60th anniversary of Chinese rule, then-Vice-president Xi Jinping pledged to speed up Tibet's economic development and to promote the idea that Han and minorities "cannot live without each other." He praised Tibet as a national security screen, referring to its role as a barrier between China and India, as an ecological screen as the source of China's major rivers, and as a source of strategic resources. A few weeks later, young monk Tsewang Norbu from Ganzi County, a Tibetan region of Sichuan, drank gasoline, poured it over himself and burned himself to death as he shouted, "We Tibetans Want Freedom, Long Live the Dalai Lama." It was the second such desperate measure within a few months. Media reported that within a year, more than 30 Tibetans had burned themselves to death or attempted to do so.

As we see from the examples of Inner Mongolia and Tibet, the Chinese state's projects of nation-building, cultural reordering, and resource extraction are intimately entwined, often resulting in problems with environmental injustice in situations where alternative identities and ethnic allegiances are perceived as threats to the dominance of the Han. In an effort to bring these regions more tightly under Beijing's sway and to integrate ethnic minority populations, even while defining their traditional cultures as backward and uncivilized, Beijing has provided a system of limited benefits through Minorities Institutes and favorable policies on birth rates, as well as a "Develop the West" policy whose impacts are debatable. The state's motivations have not only been to establish clear boundaries and buffers against potential and perceived enemies and competitors, but also to secure access to resources, including grain-lands, hydropower, minerals, fossil fuels, and timber. Local people have had little to say about whether and how these resources are used, and have seen little benefit from their extraction. In a clear and striking example of the dynamics of environmental injustice, the harms from degradation due to resource extraction have been displaced to the periphery, while environmental benefits have been enjoyed at the center.

The gaps between rich and poor, between Han and minorities, between interior and coast, are thus rooted in ethnicity, class, and above all access to resources. Whether these contradictions can be resolved will greatly affect China's prospects for "sustainable" development. A government that is committed to pursuing sustainable development must attempt to improve living standards without poisoning the country. It must attempt to demonstrate to ethnic minority groups that the national project does not disenfranchise them. It must pursue environmental equity, transparency, and rule of law. These are serious challenges for any government, especially in a world that is reaching the limits of its resources.

Unfortunately, if trends continue, the state's stated purpose, that of achieving both environmental protection and economic growth, will be little more than a cloak for repression and environmental injustice in resource-rich border areas. There is little internal debate about this, perhaps because even many thoughtful and well-educated Han Chinese tend to believe the official line that the central government has done a great deal to help these "backwards" areas; they see minorities who protest or "riot" as simply ungrateful. Educated young Han eager for travel adventure hold romantic notions about life in Tibet and Inner Mongolia, but few have much understanding of the complexity or desirability of creating a multi-ethnic society that respects cultural difference without stereotyping, exploitation, or condescension. Moreover, few of them appreciate their own roles in perpetuating such dynamics.

ENVIRONMENTAL JUSTICE: INTERNATIONAL DIMENSIONS

The final dynamic for us to consider with respect to environmental justice is the international one, with China serving as both an importer and exporter of environmental harm. In recent decades, the trend toward state-led environmental degradation has intensified and internationalized, as China's thirst for resources, from timber and wildlife to fossil fuels and minerals, has led to an increase in environmental degradation in places within and beyond national boundaries. We have already seen that as the world's manufacturing hub, China has attracted and borne the costs of pollution for many developed countries and that increasingly, within China, that pollution is being pushed out of wealthy Eastern cities and into rural areas and out to the vulnerable West. While many international corporations argue that they adhere to more stringent environmental and labor standards than do Chinese domestic companies, anti-globalization activists claim that the developing world is in a "race to the bottom" as they compete against each other for foreign capital. By 2002, one-third of China's industrial output came from factories with foreign investment, and the debate over whether such enterprises are generally positive or negative for China's environmental performance remains unresolved, with some evidence suggesting that much depends on whether the multinational corporations originate from low-standard or high-standard countries (Stalley 2010). When the problem of sub-contracting to middlemen is included, as already mentioned with respect to the shoe and iPad manufacturers targeted by Greenpeace, it becomes even more difficult to make judgments on these firms' environmental impact. Such subcontractors are often from Hong Kong or Taiwan and have been associated with sweatshop-like conditions and sub-standard pollution controls.

As we reflect on how environmental harm is displaced to the vulnerable, we would be remiss not to consider one of the most dramatic examples of how the West literally exports some of its toxics to China in the form of post-consumer waste. The electronics recycling business, which is centered in a cluster of four small villages in southern Guangdong Province near Hong Kong, has some of the highest concentrations of toxic materials in the world. This is an issue of wide discussion and mobilization for the international environmental community.

The Basel Action Network (BAN) is a non-governmental organization dedicated to exposing the environmental injustices inherent in the globalization of the toxic waste trade, and is based on the 1989 Basel Convention on the Control of Transboundary Movements of Hazardous Wastes and their Disposal. BAN activists have been working for more than a decade to stop the export of electronic wastes to China, especially from the United States. (The U.S. has signed but not ratified the Basel Convention.) International awareness of the e-waste problem was raised significantly when CBS broadcast an episode of "Sixty Minutes" about the impact of this trade on the villages of Guiyu. The villages, which once produced rice, have become a dumping ground for the world's electronic detritus. The waste arrives by the container-load via Hong Kong. Villagers disassemble and sort components from computers, televisions, cell phones, and other electronics. Many of the chemicals are highly toxic, especially when burned or soaked in acid baths during the deconstruction. Small children and even babies play in mountains of waste as their parents extract minuscule quantities of copper, gold, chips, and other valuables for a meager living. Dioxin levels in Guiyu are the world's highest, while lead, chromium, tin, PVC flame retardants (which contain dioxin and furan), and other toxics also leach into the groundwater and fall from the air. Although laws in the U.S. and other developed countries as well as China forbid the export and import of these materials, and virtuous citizens in the West often go to great lengths to ensure that their toxic electronics are disposed of in what they believe to be a responsible fashion, the illegal trade is highly lucrative and loopholes abound. Indeed, Greenpeace estimates that 50 to 80 percent of U.S. e-waste is exported, much of it to Asia, although Africa also gets its share. The U.S. EPA is cooperating with China and other developing countries to reduce the trade and find a solution (http://epa.gov/oia/toxics/ewaste.html). Greenpeace, BAN, and other NGOs are pressuring electronics manufacturers to stop using the most hazardous substances in their products and have obtained commitments from some of them. However, as the worldwide consumption of electronic products continues to explode, and the lifetimes of these products grow ever shorter with the introduction of must-have gadgets that make usable products appear to be obsolete, this problem is likely to worsen.

DEBATE ABOUT INTERNATIONAL IMPACTS

Thus far, this book has been focused primarily on how China's environmental challenges are playing out domestically. The themes we have identified in earlier chapters suggest a need for further research into how they play out in the international arena, as the country and its businesses engage, operate, and develop elsewhere in the world. How do domestic considerations affect the role of the Chinese government on the world stage? How does Chinese national identity fuel its international actions? How and where is civil society within China making transnational linkages? In terms of environmental justice and the displacement of environmental harm, we cannot ignore the external environmental consequences of China's domestic policies and it will be useful to consider the question briefly here.

China's economic growth, the rise of its middle class and its new-found position as manufacturer to the world have created an almost insatiable appetite for resources, some of which are consumed at home and some of which are transformed into products that are then sold the world over. As more Chinese enjoy higher incomes and demand a better standard of living, government and industry are casting about the globe for food, material inputs, economic partners, and markets. At the same time, China's own increasingly stringent environmental standards – particularly the country's celebrated if also flouted logging ban – have decreased damaging activities domestically, shifting pressure to other countries. As was discussed earlier, although China bans logging at home, its furniture manufacturing industry needs lumber and seeks it from forests abroad. This commodity chain exemplifies both the potential for environmental degradation and opportunities for reform in China's quest for resources (Sun et al. 2008). Decades ago, China was largely isolated from the world; today Chinese foreign aid programs and businesses are active worldwide. What this means for the environment is as yet unclear. Indeed, there is an active debate among scholars, analysts, and journalists: Does China's international quest for resources and business bode well or ill for the planet?

On the subject of foreign aid, some observers hold a surprisingly positive view. Deborah Brautigam's study, *The Dragon's Gift* (2009), suggests that Chinese projects are rebuilding Africa across sectors, providing for schools and roads as well as energy and resources infrastructure. Although a number of investments seem aimed at procuring resources – some repayments in Angola are made directly in oil – other projects, such as hospitals, are not as clearly directed at extraction. Although Chinese foreign aid balance sheets can be opaque, broad economic and strategic interests appear to remain at the heart of many of China's decisions, some of which are resource oriented, some of which are not. Nonetheless, it is clear that many projects in Latin America and the Middle East are focused on securing energy (Dittmer and Yu 2010). This may be a case of China's self-interests in markets and materials aligning with the needs of less developed countries for investment and capital; in the case of Africa that might prove positive on balance (Taylor 2009). Perhaps as a response to criticisms that China is only interested in shoring up strategic resources across the globe, the government in 2011 released a white paper demonstrating that only about five percent of its development projects are directly related to oil and mining, while more than half focus on economic infrastructure and public facilities. This point drew praise from analysts at the Worldwatch Institute (Bi 2011), who hailed China's approach as a "green aid" model for the world.

A darker viewpoint suggests that China's overseas development assistance projects are still largely focused, if subtly so, on gaining access to resources. That was the conclusion of the Congressional Research Service (Lum et al. 2009), based on an earlier, widely cited review by the Robert F. Wagner Graduate School of Public Service at New York University. Harsh critics suggest that China is engaging in a modern version of colonialism, offering foreign aid to build infrastructure like roads and ports to allow for easier extraction of resources. This is consistent with the Chinese contention that foreign aid should be mutually beneficial (Kjøllesdal and Welle-Strand 2010). Brautigam counters that China is merely helping other countries take advantage of the lessons China learned, "that their own natural resources could be assets for modernization and prosperity" (2009, p. 311).

Some Chinese business investments, as distinct from the government's foreign aid packages, point alarmingly to resource grabbing tied to traditional, harmful consumption. According to Chinese Ministry of Commerce statistics for 2010, Chinese foreign direct investment (FDI) was fifth highest in the world at close to $70 billion. Seventy percent of that was by government owned or controlled entities, with investment in the energy and mining sector at the top of the list (Ministry of Commerce 2011).

Consider a sample of investment in energy in Latin America in recent years. In 2010, China's state-owned Sinopec bought a 40 percent stake in the Brazilian unit of a Spanish oil company for $7.1 billion and purchased outright the Argentine subsidiary of a U.S. oil company for $2.45 billion; in 2011, Sinopec paid another $3.45 billion for a 30 percent share of a Portuguese oil corporation. Another state company, Sinochem, paid $3 billion for a stake in an oil field off Brazil's coast in 2010 (Ma, Wayne 2011). Even in more developed countries, Chinese companies are muscularly asserting their investment power and interests. Australian farmers in November 2011 complained to Agence France-Presse that Chinese demand for coal was pitting food and cropland in a losing battle against state-owned energy giant Shenhua (Coopes 2011). Commenting on a mining renaissance, Western Australia's Premier Colin Barnett told TIME magazine that "China's almost insatiable demand for natural resources continues to drive our economy" (Schuman 2011).

It must be noted that the lines between Chinese private companies and the government are often blurred. Companies can be state-owned or quasi-private. They are sometimes required to operate under state guidelines, but those guidelines are not well enforced. Even those who praise China's foreign assistance programs acknowledge serious problems with lax environmental standards, either on paper or as applied. Chinese companies have been implicated in illegal harvesting of timber and fish and in ignoring and even running roughshod over local communities. And while international resistance to large hydro-power projects as the cause of serious environmental harm has solidi-fied in recent decades, China continues to build dams at home and abroad. The country's Eximbank has financed such projects since 2000 in Congo, Ethiopia, Ghana, and Sudan, among others (Brautigam 2009); resistance to a Chinese dam planned for the Mekong in Myanmar was so widespread in 2011 that Myanmar's government pulled back, a surprising move for an authoritarian country heavily beholden to China.

We can see the potential for positive outcomes from China's devel-opment strategies abroad if host countries do indeed benefit from increases in aid, trade, and investment. Yet China's economic demands also present grave environmental challenges. Opening new markets and tapping resources may benefit China and its partner nations in the short run. However, they also lead to environmental degradation, as well as a tendency to flood local markets with cheap consumer goods and crowd out subsistence local traders. The spreading of the Chinese development model, which is not so different from previous centuries of Western development, raises serious concerns: Can the world sustain this? Can the planet survive such demand and conquest? One of the most important ways that we can answer this question is by refraining from painting China as all good or all bad. We must cultivate a nuanced appreciation for China's historical moment, constraints, pressures, and ambitions, and for the responsibilities of other countries. Only then are equitable solutions likely to emerge.

CONCLUSIONS

As we have seen in this chapter, the dynamics of environmental injus-tice tend to push the costs of pollution onto the most vulnerable and politically weak. A well-organized anti-pollution push in one place can result in a factory opening somewhere else; pressure to clean Beijing's air has shifted industry to outlying areas and diverted resources from other projects. Rural areas become dumping grounds for urban waste; poor countries bear the brunt of pollution for wealthy consumers. Broadly speaking, environmental harms tend to be displaced from wealthy areas to poor ones, even as resources are extracted disproportionately from remote and less developed areas to fuel economic growth for more developed countries, including China. As these tensions and contradictions become more evident in a shrinking, globalizing world of limited resources, they are focusing increasing attention on the challenge of achieving environmental justice while providing for the needs of the world's growing population.

As we conclude this chapter on environmental justice, we may wish once again to raise questions asked at the beginning of this volume: Can this trend be reversed in a world of increasing limits of resources, even as pollution "sinks," including carbon repositories like forests, are shrinking quickly? Is it even possible to build a fair and equitable world? As China's story tells us, there are signs of hope, but also room for despair. China's demand for resources is being driven not only by domestic consumers but also by international ones. As the world's manufacturing engine, China bears some of the pollution costs of the developed world's overconsumption along with the consumption and waste generated by its own rising middle class. At the same time, China has only just begun to address the material needs of the impoverished periphery in the West. For these reasons, and despite strong environmental laws and regulations, Chinese citizens are swimming in a sea of toxic pollutants. Many rivers and lakes are unusable even for irrigation; air quality is dangerously unhealthy; desertification, erosion, and dust storms are depleting arable lands. Public health costs can be measured in early death, chronic disease, lost productivity, and diminished quality of life.

There is little that the developed world can do to help China to implement its environmental laws, which, if enforced, would mitigate some of the worst effects of pollution and even have a secondary benefit of correcting trade imbalances by making Chinese goods more expensive, thereby reducing tensions between China and developed countries. Many of the challenges described in this book are for the Chinese people to solve. However, people in developed countries can engage with China in many other ways, sharing ideas, expertise, and technology and working to change behavior at home so as better to link with the developing world in common cause. This is the urgent challenge for policy makers, ordinary citizens, and readers of this book.

QUESTIONS FOR RESEARCH AND DISCUSSION

1 How should governments deal most fairly with the siting of undesirable but necessary land uses such as garbage dumps, landfills, and polluting factories? How should they ensure that people living near extracted resources enjoy benefits from the extraction?

2 How does China's treatment of minority nationalities compare to such interactions in your own country? Is China's government engaged in a form of environmental injustice, or is it simply using available resources to build the country? How would you improve China's Western Development program to create better options for sustainability and justice?

3 Compare the materials from the International Campaign for Tibet and the Chinese government (links below). How can we explain such radically different views of whether the Tibetans are benefitting from the Han presence?

4 What is the relationship between economic globalization and environmental justice, as reflected in China's trade and investment relationships with other countries?

ADDITIONAL RESOURCES

- Basel Action Network: http://www.ban.org/about/ and their report, "Exporting Harm," at http://www.ban.org/E-waste/technotrashfinalcomp.pdf
- China Digital Times map of cancer villages: http://chinadigitaltimes.net/2009/05/a-map-of-chinas-cancer-villages/
- China Tibet Online (government publication): http://eng.tibet.cn/ and Chinese government whitepaper on Tibet: http://www.china.org.cn/e-white/tibet/index.htm
- Human Rights Watch report on lead poisoning: http://www.hrw.org/reports/2011/06/15/my-children-have-been-poisoned
- International Campaign for Tibet: http://www.savetibet.org/
- "Sixty Minutes" 2008 story on electronic waste in Guiyu: http://www.cbsnews.com/stories/2008/11/06/60minutes/main4579229.shtml
- Southern Mongolian Human Rights Information Center: http://www.smhric.org/

7 | Prospects for the Future ————

In only a generation and a half, China has undergone a transition that now touches every conceivable facet of the country, including the government, the people, civil society, and even intangible cultural characteristics such as identity and tradition. China's rapid economic and much slower political "openings" have drastically changed the landscape, both physically and metaphorically, in ways that could not have been imagined a few decades ago. As we look at present-day China and wonder about the future of its environment, it is easy to be overwhelmed by the enormity of the country's strengths and challenges. How do we begin to draw conclusions? What is the path forward?

From the exposition and analysis in the preceding pages, one fact is clear: China's environment is beset by numerous interconnected and countervailing forces and pressures. This book has attempted to analyze the trends on the ground today, outline the challenges the country faces, and describe where the government and society are facing setbacks or making advances. We have examined the environmental challenges posed by many aspects of China's present situation, including its astronomical growth, the evolving role of the state, and the emergence of civil society. At the same time we have seen that progress toward a sustainable future is hampered by an East-West divide, unequal access to resources, corruption, lax enforcement of regulations, and unresolved and often unacknowledged ethnic conflicts. Even the progress made by middle class and green activists can be illusory if the environmental problems that are tackled in one region are simply exported to another region of China, or another country entirely. These themes intersect and overlap, complement and reinforce, exacerbate and diminish one another in complex ways. To understand one, we need to understand them all.

Consider, for example, the demographic question. Discussion of the country's population size was politically taboo during the Mao years, but since then both government and society have openly acknowledged that it is a powerful constraint on China's development. While debate continues about the growth of the world's most populous nation – including the effect of relaxations of the contentious One Child policy – the sheer number of people and their demands are a powerful force limiting China's choices. At the heart of the country's development is the struggle to bring wealth and comfort to more than one billion people, many of whom have lived in poverty for generations. One cannot overstate the pressure that this scale of poverty brings on leaders' decision making. Certainly, China has been able to take advantage of globalization, becoming a manufacturer to the world and expanding its economy drastically. The chances are good that anyone reading this book has something made in China within arm's reach at this very moment. However, with this rising wealth, China's new middle class now demands clean air and water even as its material desires spell trouble for the environment, a contradictory impulse that is not easy for government leaders to accommodate.

The primary response of the government to demands for better living standards has been liberalization and decentralization of economic controls, yet this causes an immense quandary for China's authoritarian state system. Yes, loosening economic restrictions has created conditions for spectacular growth, lifting millions out of poverty. The central government ceded some of its power in a bid to expand the economy; in essence, the state was able to catalyze China's economic turnaround precisely because it had such top-down control to relinquish. However, the "economic miracle" that raised incomes and the national GDP is now also a curse, as the state struggles to limit further destruction of China's limited natural resources and begin to clean up the mess generated by decades of environmental abuse. Officials have recognized growing levels of environmental harm – stemming partly from a sense of lawlessness among middle-level officials and industrial leaders – and they have instituted world-class environmental regulations. But these laws are poorly enforced. The *de facto* reality remains woefully behind the ideal. This implementation gap stems at least in part from a political and social conflict between Western-style economic growth and a healthy environment. For example, China today sees deforestation as a problem that creates flooding at home; it bans logging in sensitive river headwaters but simultaneously fosters a manufacturing sector that supplies the furniture needs of consumers an ocean away. Thus, the government essentially looks the other way as domestic forests continue to be cut and as timber enters – often illegally – from ravaged forests in Southeast Asia, Russia, and Africa. Water use is a similar arena where the state appears torn between conflicting goals. The massive South-North water transfer is an example. Intended to relieve water shortages in the East, the project will cause dislocation and hardship for local populations and, activists argue, could create environmental problems and increase tensions with surrounding countries whose major rivers will be affected by the plan. What is more, beyond its borders, China has largely refused to cooperate in regional, transboundary management schemes for the numerous rivers that originate in its territory.

The juggernaut that is globalization is the force behind many of China's environmental woes. But globalization can also be a source of hope and a stimulus for innovation. China continues to make strides in developing and producing clean technology; in particular, it invests heavily in areas like solar and wind energy, clean car technology, and desalinization plants, positioning the country to reap profits in the global economy in the future. Perhaps this represents an alternative, realistic path for the future development of China, one where economic and environmental incentives could align. We can see evidence that China is moving in this direction as Chinese civil society groups exercise their new rights to participate in environmental decisions, express their views in the media, and take part in demonstrations, even at times with the blessings of the government. But even as these civil society actors assume a more significant role, their size and effectiveness remain constrained. The Chinese Communist Party remains concerned about social unrest that could challenge central authority, and so it closely monitors and controls modern social movements. Recent history for China has included dark periods of isolation. The openness mandated by a globalized society and modern Internet communication is still viewed with a wary eye, as the government attempts to regulate the flow of ideas while remaining open to the world. The state is in essence performing a high-wire act, balancing the need for centralized control and the suppression of protest against the need for more public participation, more transparency, and greater reliance on the rule of law. A particularly interesting area to monitor for signs of progress in this direction will be the evolving judicial system; its independence will be tested as civil society begins to test the laws and their new rights through the courts. Meanwhile, NGOs must tread carefully, asserting their rights, voicing grievances, and lobbying officials and the media without angering the state so much as to provoke a crackdown.

Emerging civil society also faces questions about its own ability and intent, as it intersects in unusual ways with China's changing demographics and economy. A newly empowered middle class is beginning to demand more of the government with respect to food safety and pollution standards. The middle-class Chinese environmental movement is growing, as evidenced by routine news reports of mass incidents protesting pollution and harmful development. Chinese cities have become cleaner as community groups and loosely organized citizens confront government planners and businesspeople. Some measure of justice has been meted out to corrupt industry barons and officials. At the same time, at least some of these demands also stem from broader popular desires for more consumption and affluence, both of which accompany a lifestyle that contributes to environmental degradation. So, while ENGOs press the government for action, they also need to do some soul searching. Can the environmental movement advocate an alternate path and still draw support from a middle class that at times is focused on wealth and conspicuous consumption? Successful protests against polluters may shut down a factory, only to cause it to relocate in a more marginal, less powerful community. Severe environmental problems are occurring in ethnic minority communities on the periphery of the country, where a grab for resources is thinly disguised as a development program. In these hinterlands, poor people will bear the heaviest burden of climate change. Yet these communities suffer racial and class prejudices. This will be an evolving area for China's burgeoning environmental movement as it seeks to balance the desires of its urban support base and wider ideals of environmental justice.

A clear case can be made that the national government – or some parts of it – is inching toward a greater alliance with the green movement, as part of an overall trend toward an expanded civil society and rule-by-law. Top government officials have recognized that cleaning up the environment requires a combination of clear laws, transparent standards and practices, development of institutions, defined rights, a democratic process, encouragement of public participation, and engagement with the media. Environmental protection official Pan Yue's 2006 comments about expanding and supporting the "non-political" environmental movement as an experiment in democracy support this idea. As Qu Geping states in the documentary "Waking the Green Tiger," environmental regulation in any part of the world requires, "supervision from the bottom up." Top-down efforts are important, but some form of green democracy is essential. Additional reforms are needed to encourage such groups and give them more breadth, depth, clout, and legal protections. Western students, activists, organizations, and individuals can find more ways to engage with and support these groups, who have a tough task as they attempt to shift powerful forces toward a different path.

Chinese people have powerful motivations for improving the quality of their lives. The older generation has not forgotten the days of extreme poverty, grueling labor, and sacrifice in the face of famine and death, while younger Chinese are eager to join the world and enjoy their lives. But we can see a cultural complication in China's development and use of its natural resources that stems from the country's national identity and genealogical story of a homogeneous culture that was once the envy of the world. Woven into the cultural fabric of the nation is pride in its former status as the vaunted Middle Kingdom. Neither consumer nor political choices can be divorced from the burden of generations of ingrained insecurity about the global stature of their country. Today, Chinese strongly desire to reassert status – to gain face, as it were – and finally have the means to do so, having benefited from China's economic transformation and the forces of globalization. Yet this insecurity may also threaten to overheat the economy, overwhelm the environment, and power ruinous consumption. As the country strives to improve its standing in the world and bolster the quality of life for more than one billion people, much of its development generates environmental harm. Incentives to correct course are not readily available when that harm is displaced – to the margins of communities, to rural areas, to the periphery of the country, or outside its borders. We see this preoccupation with face materialized in the predilection for grand construction projects and development. Some of these developments can be understood as legitimate ways to expand a developing economy and alleviate poverty, but others come with tremendous environmental costs. How such tensions are resolved can have grave consequences for the environment and human security, as we have seen in the construction of the controversial Three Gorges Dam and the plan to transfer water from the South to the North. Again, here we see an alternative path for China: Can the country pursue prestige and power by leading the way in sustainable development and technology?

A long history of public distrust of central authority also frustrates the government's ability to address challenges. Chinese citizens have a history of circumventing and subverting regulations through bribery. The traditional practice of respecting hierarchies and of seeking relief through the influence of someone more powerful dates back to the time of the emperors. This tendency was exacerbated during the Mao years and during the reforms that followed. During Mao's time, private property and personal wealth were abhorred so individual citizens had few opportunities to inflict personal damage on the environment. The extensive damage that did occur, as described earlier, was directed from the top down. After 1978, when "getting rich" was embraced by Deng Xiaoping, the grip of the state relaxed. But there were few rules in place and few mechanisms to prevent China's new entrepreneurs from saving money by exploiting resources and dumping wastes. Regulations, when they were passed, were circumvented. In the old days it was the emperor who lived far away, and was unable to enforce edicts. In the new China, it is the regulators who are distant and ineffectual. Even as law enforcement gradually improves, this dynamic still gives rise to localized instances of intense pollution of public lands and waterways and high-profile incidents like the 2008 melamine scandal. Individuals and small factories are not the only ones to avoid regulation. Even China's largest corporations, like Huaneng and Huadian Power, have been caught repeatedly and fined for failing to obtain environmental permits before commencing work on dams in the Upper Yangzi.

Asserting the rule of law and creating an ethos where Chinese citizens feel empowered to help preserve and enjoy a clean environment will require enormous effort. Ancient and traditional beliefs and institutions – Confucianism, Daoism, and Buddhism – may provide some guidance. They each speak to the need to promote sustainable relationships, harmony, and respect for the non-human world. But for many young Chinese who find themselves cut off from the past, growing up in an intensely materialist and non-religious country, these traditions carry little weight. Fortunately, other traditions can be invoked. Environmental groups emphasize a love of nature for its own sake, encouraging nature walks, photography, tree planting, and preservation of wild lands, rivers, and animals. You do not have to be a philosopher to admire a golden monkey or a panda. Social justice, distributive justice, the rights of individuals and minorities, and the desire to project China as a leading and positive force in the world are also powerful sentiments that underpin the revolution and form part of a patriotic identity. If these new convictions and older traditions are combined, could they prevail in the face of corruption, materialism, and a central government deeply suspicious of political and social movements? Some activists and even officials suggest that it is possible and inevitable, because the alternative is unsustainable.

Finally, we must consider the complex challenge posed by the East-West divide. Vast areas of western China, home to rural peasants and ethnic minorities, remain relatively untouched by the modernization and growing wealth of the East. The China of Beijing or Shanghai is a vastly different place from Tibet or Inner Mongolia or even the rural farming areas of the country. In these areas life has changed little and in some places basic needs remain unsatisfied. People living in these areas remain excluded from much of China's development, disconnected from the country's gleaming cities and rise to prominence. The sheer numbers of poor give impetus to the state's growth and development targets. But the poor tend to benefit least, as wealth trickles too slowly from the urban megapolis to the rural village, and income inequalities worsen with every passing year. When we take a closer look at these regions, we suspect that government attempts to "develop" infrastructure are often no more than strategies to extract natural resources at the expense of a minority, marginalized population. Development campaigns, and even some environmental campaigns like the restoration of the grasslands discussed earlier, may also result in the dislocation of minorities or enforced assimilation as entire communities are broken up. Meanwhile, as environmental movements in the wealthy East grow stronger, much environmental harm is simply displaced to the periphery. In some cases, this practice undermines the government's legitimacy and fuels ongoing struggles that threaten China's stability.

Although the evidence presented in this book does not suggest that China has reached a point of no return in terms of environmental degradation, taken together, the environmental challenges suggest that China, its government, and its people will have to grapple with a long list of questions as they attempt to build what they call a harmonious and sustainable society:

- What is the ultimate goal of China's economic development model? Can the country afford a trajectory modeled on that of the West? Can the rest of the world afford that?
- Where does the state fit into the picture of environmental governance? Does the state have the political will or ability to eschew a develop-at-all-costs mentality?
- What is the path ahead for China's homegrown, if somewhat nascent, environmental movement? Can it be inclusive without compromising values? Who does it ultimately represent? Can it challenge the government or business effectively? Can it form and maintain useful relationships with the international environmental movement?
- Can the Chinese people search their souls during their quest for an improved quality of life? Can they avoid the excesses of the Global North that displaced so much environmental harm onto the developing South? Can they collectively choose an alternative

development model that might rest on post-materialist values emphasizing self-expression and the construction of a meaningful life over material consumption?

- Is China's model addressing wider issues of injustice and oppression of poor, marginalized, and minority voices? Or is this economic model only contributing to further exploitation of those who live at the margins? What would greater inclusion do for China and its people?

- Where does the international community fit in? Where does China fit into the international community? If the environment is truly a global issue, does the world not have a responsibility to China and vice versa? What lessons does China have to offer the rest of the world? If China is greening itself, is it doing so at the cost of vulnerable populations elsewhere in the world?

Answers to these questions will not come easily. Complex challenges within China overlap and intersect in ways that rule out quick fixes. And while there are clear reasons for hope, time is running short. As we have seen in the preceding chapters, the choices China is facing are extremely difficult. There is huge pressure for China to continue on its current path of rapid growth coupled with environmental degradation, both within and beyond borders. The ability to shift course is constrained by historical and cultural baggage that puts the emphasis on global recognition and conspicuous consumption.

There are encouraging signs that a shift is already under way, with greater confidence in the legal system, increased public participation and information transparency, and broad recognition that development that chokes and harms is undesirable. Significant forces are working tirelessly for greater attention to and emphasis on sustainability, including within the Chinese state system. As we have seen, China and the world are so intertwined that what happens in China not only impacts all of us, but what all of us do has an impact in China. Through our buying habits, political action in our home countries, information sharing, and other choices that we make every day, we can join with those in China working for a sustainable future. Yet if China's policy makers, corporations, and politically powerful middle class, along with other global actors and each one of us through our individual decisions, continue to displace harms onto yet more vulnerable populations and future generations, then joined together as we are as a planet, we will continue to accumulate debt that can never be repaid.

FINAL THOUGHTS

Here are a few reflections with which to conclude this investigation of China's environmental challenges. Today, we know much more than we did even 30 years ago about the dynamics of the global ecosystems that sustain us. Wherever we live, we are connected to China, and to each other. We share air, water, food, oceans, wildlife, agricultural harvests, and toxic wastes. We are dependent on each other for the food, shelter, and the material objects that make our lives more comfortable and interesting. We have learned, slowly, to recognize the priceless and invisible services that our ecosystems provide, from water purification to carbon fixation to pollination. We understand the importance of the variety of life species, from charismatic megafauna like Siberian tigers and pandas to the humble and tiny sea creatures that build the reefs that nurture the fish that feed us. With and without religion, we have been able to find inspiration and renewal in the natural world. As communities, we find meaning in our greater understanding of the capacity of all creatures, human and non-human, to communicate and to seek lives free from suffering. Yet we also urgently mourn our losses: the disappearance each day of the last surviving member of a species, the disturbing news about rapidly melting polar ice and sea-level rise even more dramatic than first feared, the noticeably more frequent severe weather events such as droughts and cyclones.

Collectively, we feel deeply uneasy at the apparent inadequacy of the state system to deal with global and transboundary challenges such as climate change or the illegal trade in endangered species. Where treaties have been signed and ratified, weak implementation and enforcement suggest that the agreements are unequal to the magnitude of the challenges we face. We understand that the predictable and progressive collapse of ecosystems and the degradation of the global environment within the lifetimes of some of those already born are linked to the inability of national governments to act, to an exploding human population, and to a relentless economic globalization that unleashes forces difficult to control. The world's thirst for limited natural resources such as fossil fuels, minerals, timber, and fish has sparked fierce international competition and new sources of conflict. This is the "resource curse" that sometimes turns resource-rich but politically weak developing nations into battlefields for external powers and multinational businesses competing for access to the materials that feed economic growth and profits at the expense of local populations and the environment.

We recognize that there is something profoundly wrong with the way we are doing business as a planet. We need to reject the drive for economic growth at all costs and establish a different concept of security – human, state, and global – that is linked to respect for the limitations of the planet's non-renewable resources. As the United Nations Environment Programme argues, we must "decouple" the planet's quest for prosperity from its unsustainable use of resources (Fischer-Kowalski and Swilling 2011). We must also understand that the "ecological footprint" of a nation can be correctly measured only by considering international as well as domestic extraction of resources; so too with the disposal of pollution and toxic waste. All environmental problems are ultimately globally shared; we can neither export them nor build a protective wall to keep them out. We need to create the political space to allow countries like China to perform better, to satisfy them that developed countries are doing their fair share to deal with the problems for which industrial societies are primarily responsible. At the same time, the world needs to help developing countries to curb some of the worst impacts of the pollution and climate change that will ultimately be felt most sharply among the world's poor. In international environmental law, this concept is enshrined in the principle of "common but differentiated responsibilities," which acknowledges that we have a shared interest in dealing with the globe's enormous environmental challenges, but that the developed world needs to go first to resolve the problems, and it needs to help the developing world to pay for its transformation to a cleaner, more sustainable development model. The "right to development" is also a powerful principle of international environmental law, and the globe must find ways to respect this. China could, indeed it must, be a modern laboratory for designing a new path. As we have seen, China holds a special place on the world environmental stage. In so many ways, China's route to the future will be that of the planet.

China observers these days often fall into two camps: critics and apologists. Yet this book has called for a more nuanced response. To deal with China we need to see the whole picture, good and bad, and think strategically about how to boost the promise and minimize the peril. The concepts around which this book has been organized may help readers in the developed world to reflect on how we can support China in this effort. In terms of governance, we can support the actors within the central government who are trying to "green" the country's administrative patterns by acknowledging and praising them in international forums, providing international expertise to help them craft win-win solutions that will gain wide acceptance by the laggards within the bureaucracy, and strengthen their efforts to spread rule of law by continuing the academic and governmental exchanges that have already borne so much fruit. We can remove obstacles to the transfer and dissemination of clean technology and create strong international mechanisms to help China, and the rest of the developing world, avoid exacerbating the global environmental crisis for which we in the developed world are largely responsible. In terms of national identity, we can engage in the discussion by sharing resources about other nations' struggles with these questions, include Chinese scholars in debates about culture and sustainability, encourage publication in Chinese of relevant books and documents, and try to foster a sense that an international community is together searching for ways to shift human culture from one of exploitation of nature to one of respect and care. In terms of civil society, we can support Chinese citizens' groups by providing opportunities for their leaders to travel overseas to network with their peers, attend international negotiations, study abroad, and obtain resources to fund their activities. We can also support those who have been subjected to political repression by raising their names in international forums and encouraging the Chinese government to permit more space for free expression and public participation. Finally, in terms of equity and the displacement of harm, we can become more sensitive to problems of environmental justice across time, space, and species, considering the impacts of global consumption patterns on resource extraction and waste disposal, and understanding more clearly how the negative externalities of these activities tend to harm the most vulnerable, both human and non-human. While awareness of the ethical dimensions of our behavior will not in itself shift us away from destructive patterns, it may bring to light what has been hidden and make it more difficult to pursue the old ways.

True security will come not from foreign wars or expansion of overseas influence in an effort to secure the last few generations' worth of the earth's treasures. Rather, it will come from tapping energy and using products derived close to home, through the wide-scale adoption of renewable technologies and reusable materials. In national planning, we must move toward what ecological economist Herman Daly (1996) has called a "steady-state economy," while making allowances for other countries that cannot yet do so; in production, we must move toward what architect William McDonough and chemist Michael Braungart (2002) call "cradle-to-cradle" lifecycles, such that once taken from the earth, resources can be used over and over again, forever.

Making this transition will take tremendous political will and effort. It will require leadership from China, the U.S., and Europe, from developed and developing countries, from the Global North and the Global South. It must come from each individual, from each community, from each province, and from each nation. The goal is development that truly benefits all citizens, with healthy air and water, rich forests and jungles that are home to a biodiversity of animals, plants, birds, and insects, urban parks where citizens can reconnect to nature, and human lives whose meanings are measured not by material consumption or possessions but by compassion, connection to others, and reverence for life.

References

Anderson, Benedict (1983) *Imagined Communities: Reflections on the Origin and Spread of Nationalism.* London: Verso.

Atsmon, Yuval; Dixit, Vinay; Leibowitz, Glenn; and Wu, Cathy (2011) *Understanding China's Growing Love for Luxury.* McKinsey Insights China [online]. Available at: http://www.mckinsey.com/locations/greaterchina/InsightsChina_LuxuryGoods.pdf (accessed January 7, 2012).

Auffhammer, Maximilian and Carson, Richard T. (2008) Forecasting the path of China's CO_2 emissions using province-level information. *Journal of Environmental Economics and Management,* 55(3): 229–47.

Avedon, John (1984) *In Exile from the Land of Snows: The Definitive Account of the Dalai Lama and Tibet since the Chinese Conquest.* New York: Knopf.

Bai, Xuemei (2008) The urban transition in China: Trends, consequences and policy implications. In: Martine, George; McGranahan, Gordon; Montgomery, Mark; and Fernández-Castilla, Rogelio (eds), *The New Global Frontier: Urbanization, Poverty and Environment in the 21st Century.* London: Routledge.

Balk, Deborah; McGranahan, Gordon; and Anderson, Bridget (2007) Rising tide: Assessing the risks of climate change and human settlements in low elevation coastal zones. *Environment & Urbanization,* 19(1): 17–37.

Bauer, Joanne (ed.) (2006) *Forging Environmentalism: Justice, Livelihood and Contested Environments.* Armonk, NY: M.E. Sharpe.

Becker, Jasper (1997) *Hungry Ghosts: Mao's Secret Famine.* New York: Free Press.

Bi, Jiajing (2011) China's "green aid" offers lessons for the world. *Revolt: The Worldwatch Institute's Climate and Energy Blog.* [online] April 29, 2011. Available at: http://blogs.worldwatch.org/revolt/china's-"green-aid"-offers-lessons-for-the-world/ (accessed January 7, 2012).

Blaikie, Piers (1985) *Political Economy of Soil Erosion in Developing Countries.* London: Longman.

Bookchin, Murray (1980) *Toward an Ecological Society.* Montreal: Black Rose Books.

Bradsher, Keith (2009) China's incinerators loom as global hazard. *The New York Times*. [online] August 11, 2009. Available at: http://www.nytimes.com/2009/08/12/business/energy-environment/12incinerate.html?pagewanted=all (accessed January 7, 2012).

Brandon, John J. (2011) Water: quenching the thirst for security? *In Asia*. [online] June 22, 2011. Available at http://asiafoundation.org/in-asia/2011/06/22/water-quenching-the-thirst-for-security (accessed January 7, 2012).

Brautigam, Deborah (2009) *The Dragon's Gift: The Real Story of China in Africa*. New York: Oxford University Press.

Brettell, Anna (2008) Channeling dissent: the institutionalization of environmental compliant resolution in China. In: Ho, Peter and Edmonds, Richard L. (eds). *China's Embedded Activism: Opportunities and Constraints of a Social Movement*. London: Routledge.

Brown, Lester (1995) *Who Will Feed China? Wake Up Call for a Small Planet*. New York: W.W. Norton & Co.

Central European University Center for Environmental Policy and Law (2007) *Making the Case for Environmental Justice in Central and Eastern Europe*. Budapest: Central European University. Available at: http://www.cepl.ceu.hu/system/files/ceu_teljes_pdf.pdf (accessed January 7, 2012).

Chellaney, Brahma (2011) *Water: Asia's New Battleground*. Washington, DC: Georgetown University Press.

China Daily (2011a) China to ease NGO registration policy. *China Daily*. [online] July 11, 2011. Available at: http://www.chinadaily.com.cn/china/2011-07/11/content_12878662.htm (accessed January 5, 2012).

China Daily (2011b) Change to urban identity. *China Daily*. [online] December 21, 2011. Available at: http://www.chinadaily.com.cn/opinion/2011-12/21/content_14297927.htm (accessed January 7, 2012).

China Radio International (2011) New garbage incinerator planned in Haidian. *CRI English*. [online] January 20, 2011. Available at: http://english.cri.cn/6909/2011/01/20/2743s616531.htm (accessed January 7, 2012).

Chinese Academy of Social Sciences (2008) Chinese Academy of Social Sciences Urban Development and Environment Research Center, China Urban Development Report [*Zhongguo shehui kexueyuan chengshi fazhan yu huanjing yanjiu zhongxin, Zhongguo chengshi fazhan baogao*]. [online]. Available at: http://unpan1.un.org/intradoc/groups/public/documents/APCITY/UNPAN030130.pdf (accessed January 7, 2012).

CLSA Asia-Pacific Markets (2011) China to become the world's largest market for luxury goods over the next decade. Press release. [online] June 18, 2009. Available at: https://www.clsa.com/about-clsa/media-centre/

2011-media-releases/china-to-become-the-worlds-largest-market-for-luxury-goods.php (accessed January 7, 2012).

Congressional-Executive Commission on China (2011) Annual Reports. Available at: http://www.cecc.gov (accessed January 7, 2012).

Coopes, Amy (2011) Farming Australia takes on China Inc. *Agence France-Presse.* [online] November 1, 2011. Available at: http://www.google.com/hosted-news/afp/article/ALeqM5g_PySA1n7uD1HSIZMvFhdDu2KXGg?docId=CNG.4d3e3192983c9038907dfe85d0f868e0.581 (accessed January 7, 2012).

Crooks, Robert; Nygard, Joseph; Zhang, Qingfeng; and Liu, Feng (2001) *China: Air, Land, and Water: Environmental Priorities for a New Millennium.* World Bank. [online]. Available at: http://econ.worldbank.org/external/default/main?pagePK=64165259&theSitePK=469372&piPK=64165421&menuPK=64166093&entityID=000310607_20070726151204 (accessed January 7, 2012).

Dai, Qing (1994) *Yangtze! Yangtze!* Adams, Patricia and Thibodeau, John (eds); translated from the Chinese by Nancy Liu. London, Toronto: Earthscan.

Dai, Qing (1998) *River dragon has come! The Three Gorges Dam and the Fate of China's Yangtze River and Its People.* Thibodeau, John and Williams, Philip (eds); translated from the Chinese by Yi Ming. Armonk, NY: M.E. Sharpe.

Dalai Lama XIV (1990) *Freedom in Exile.* London: Hodder and Stoughton.

Daly, Herman (1996) *Beyond Growth: The Economics of Sustainable Development.* Boston, MA: Beacon Press.

Dasgupta, Dipak (1997) *China Engaged: Integration with the Global Economy.* World Bank. [online]. Available at: http://econ.worldbank.org/external/default/main?pagePK=64165259&theSitePK=469372&piPK=64165421&menuPK=64166093&entityID=000009265_3980312102733 (accessed January 7, 2012).

Dauvergne, Peter (1997) *Shadows in the Forest: Japan and the Politics of Timber in Southeast Asia.* Cambridge, MA: MIT Press.

Diamond, Larry (2009) *The Spirit of Democracy: The Struggle to Build Free Societies Throughout the World.* New York: Times Books.

Dikötter, Frank (2010) *Mao's Great Famine: The History of China's Most Devastating Catastrophe, 1958–1962.* New York: Walker and Company.

Dittmer, Lowell and Yu, George, T. (eds) (2010) *China, the Developing World and the New Global Dynamic.* London: Lynne Rienner Publishers.

Economy, Elizabeth C. (2004) *River Runs Black: The Environmental Challenge to China's Future.* Ithaca, NY: Cornell University Press.

Ehrlich, Paul and Holdren, John T. (1971) Impact of population growth. *Science,* 171(3977): 1212–17.

Evasdottir, Erika (2004) *Obedient Autonomy: Chinese Intellectuals and the Achievement of Orderly Life*. Vancouver: University of British Columbia Press.

Fairley, Peter (2009) China's potent wind potential: Forecasters see no need for new coal and nuclear power plants. *Technology Review*. [online] September 14, 2009 Available at: http://www.technologyreview.com/energy/23460/?a-f (accessed January 7, 2012).

Fischer-Kowalski, Marina and Swilling, Mark (2011) *Decoupling: Natural Resource Use and Environmental Impacts from Economic Growth*. United Nations Environment Programme. [online]. Available at: http://www.unep.org/resourcepanel/decoupling/files/pdf/Decoupling_Report_English.pdf (accessed January 7, 2012).

Forbes (2011) *The World's Billionaires*. [online]. Available at: http://www.forbes.com/wealth/billionaires/list?country=99&industry=-1&state= (accessed January 7, 2012).

Fortune, CNN and Money (2011) *Global 500*. [online]. Available at: http://money.cnn.com/magazines/fortune/global500/2011/full_list/index.html (accessed January 7, 2012).

Freeman, Carla (2011) Quenching the dragon's thirst. *China Environment Forum*. [online]. Available at: http://www.circleofblue.org/waternews/wp-content/uploads/2011/03/Quenching-the-Dragon's-Thirst.pdf (accessed January 7, 2012).

Friends of Nature and Chinese Academy of Social Sciences (2007–2011, multiple volumes), *China Environment Yearbook*. Leiden: Brill.

Friends of Nature, Institute of Public & Environmental Affairs, Green Beagle, Envirofriends and Green Stone Environmental Action Network (2011) *The Other Side of Apple II: Pollution Spreads through Apple's Supply Chain*. [online]. Available at: http://www.ipe.org.cn/Upload/Report-IT-V-Apple-II.pdf (accessed January 7, 2012).

Fu, Jing (2010) Urban-rural income gap widest since reform. *China Daily*. [online] March 2, 2010. Available at: http://www.chinadaily.com.cn/china/2010-03/02/content_9521611.htm (accessed January 5, 2012).

Gao, Qingzhu; Li, Yu'e; Wan, Yunfan; Lin, Erda; Xiong, Wei; Jiangcun, Wangzha; Wang, Baoshan; and Li, Wenfu (2006) Grassland degradation in Northern Tibet based on remote sensing data. *Journal of Geographical Sciences*, 16(2): 165–73.

Geertz, Clifford (1973) *Interpretation of Cultures*. New York: Basic Books.

Goodman, Peter and Finn, Peter (2007) Corruption stains timber trade. *Washington Post*. [online] April 1, 2007. Available at: http://www.washingtonpost.com/wp-dyn/content/article/2007/03/31/AR2007033101287.html?nav=rss_world/asia (accessed January 7, 2012).

Gramsci, Antonio (1991) *Prison Notebooks.* New York: Columbia University Press.

Gries, Peter Hays (2005) *China's New Nationalism: Pride, Politics, and Diplomacy.* Berkeley, CA: University of California Press.

Harrell, Stevan (1997) *Cultural Encounters on China's Ethnic Frontiers.* Seattle, WA: University of Washington Press.

Harris, Richard (2010) Rangeland degradation on the Qinghai-Tibetan plateau: A review of the evidence of its magnitude and causes. *Journal of Arid Environments,* 74(1): 1–12.

Hertsgaard, Mark (1998) *Earth Odyssey: Around the World in Search of Our Environmental Future.* New York: Broadway Books.

Hessel, Dieter T. and Ruether, Rosemary Radford (eds) (2000) *Christianity and Ecology: Seeking the Well-Being of Earth and Humans.* Cambridge, MA: Harvard University Center for the Study of World Religions.

Hildebrandt, Timothy (2011) Personal communication, June 19, 2011.

Human Rights Watch (2011) *My Children Have Been Poisoned: A Public Health Crisis in Four Chinese Provinces.* [online]. Available at: http://www.hrw.org/sites/default/files/reports/china0611WebInside_0_0.pdf (accessed January 7, 2012).

Immerzeel, Walter W.; van Beek, Ludovicus P.H.; and Bierkens, Marc F.P. (2010) Climate change will affect the Asian Water Towers. *Science,* 328(5984): 1382–85.

International Rivers Network (n.d., a) *South-North Water Transfer Project.* [online]. Available at: http://www.internationalrivers.org/en/china/south-north-water-transfer-project (accessed January 7, 2012).

International Rivers Network (n.d., b) *Nu (Salween) River.* [online]. Available at: http://www.internationalrivers.org/china/nu-salween-river (accessed January 7, 2012).

Jacobs, Andrew (2011) The privileges of China's elite include purified air. *The New York Times.* [online] November 4, 2011. Available at: http://www.nytimes.com/2011/11/05/world/asia/the-privileges-of-chinas-elite-include-purified-air.html (accessed January 7, 2012).

Jahiel, Abigail (1997) Contradictory impact of reform on environmental protection in China. *China Quarterly,* 149: 83–103.

Jahiel, Abigail (1998) Organization of environmental protection in China. *China Quarterly,* 156: 757–87.

J.D. Power and Associates (2011) Global automotive outlook for 2011 appears positive as mature auto markets recover, emerging markets continue to expand. Press release. [online] February 15, 2011. Available at: http://businesscenter.

jdpower.com/news/pressrelease.aspx?ID=2011018 (accessed January 7, 2012).

Jiang, Rong (2008) *Wolf Totem*. Translated from the Chinese by Howard Goldblatt. New York: Penguin Press.

Johnson, Ian (2011) Train wreck in China heightens unease on safety standards. *The New York Times*. [online] July 24, 2011. Available at: http://www.nytimes.com/2011/07/25/world/asia/25train.html (accessed January 7, 2012).

Johnson, Todd M.; Liu, Feng; and Newfarmer, Richard (1997) *Clear Water, Blue Skies: China's Environment in the New Century*. World Bank. [online]. Available at: http://www.worldbank.org/research/1997/09/694613/clear-water-blue-skies-chinas-environment-new-century (accessed January 7, 2012).

Kahn, Joseph and Yardley, Jim (2007) Choking on growth: A series of articles and multimedia examining China's pollution crisis. *The New York Times*. [online] Multiple dates. Available at: http://www.nytimes.com/interactive/2007/08/26/world/asia/choking_on_growth.html (accessed on January 7, 2012).

Keck, Margaret E. and Sikkink, Kathryn (1998) *Activists beyond Borders: Advocacy Networks in International Politics*. Ithaca, NY: Cornell University Press.

Kjøllesdal, Kristian and Welle-Strand, Anne (2010) Foreign aid strategies: China taking over? *Asian Social Science*, 6(10): 3–13.

Klugman, Jeni (2011) *Human Development Report 2011 Sustainability and Equity: A Better Future for All*. United Nations Development Programme. [online]. Available at: http://hdr.undp.org/en/media/HDR_2011_EN_Complete.pdf (accessed January 7, 2012).

Krishnan, Ananth (2011) An enlightened hue to protests in China. *The Hindu*. [online] August 16, 2011. Available at: http://www.thehindu.com/news/international/article2359569.ece (accessed January 7, 2012).

LaFraniere, Sharon (2011) Lead poisoning in China: The hidden scourge. *The New York Times*. [online] June 15, 2011. Available at: http://www.nytimes.com/2011/06/15/world/asia/15lead.htm (accessed January 7, 2012).

Lam, Cory (2011) 12th five year plan hailed as "greenest FYP in China's history." *China Briefing*. [online] April 12, 2011. Available at http://www.china-briefing.com/news/2011/04/05/12th-five-year-plan-hailed-as-greenest-fyp-in-chinas-history.html (accessed January 7, 2012).

Li, Jing (2011) Green industries to add millions of jobs. *China Daily*. [online] November 16, 2011. Available at: http://www.chinadaily.com.cn/business/greenchina/2011-11/16/content_14113792.htm (accessed January 7, 2012).

Liang, Heng and Judith Shapiro (1983) *Son of the Revolution*. New York: Alfred A. Knopf.

Lieberthal, Kenneth (2003) *Governing China: From Revolution through Reform*, 2nd edn. New York: W.W. Norton.

Link, Perry (1992) *Evening Chats in Beijing: Probing China's Predicament.* New York: Norton.

Liu, Binyan (1990) *A Higher Kind of Loyalty: A Memoir by China's Foremost Journalist.* New York: Pantheon Books.

Liu, Lee (2010) Made in China: Cancer villages. *Environment: Science and Policy for Sustainable Development,* 52(2): 8–21.

Loh, Christine (2011) Contrasting realities: China's environmental challenge. *China Rights Forum No. 1 & 2 – China at a Crossroads.* [online]. Available at: http://hrichina.org/crf/article/5423 (accessed January 7, 2012).

Lowe, Justin (1992) Scorched earth: China's assault on Tibet's environment. *Multinational Monitor,* 13(10): 15–19.

Lü, Zhi and Turner, Jennifer (2006) Building a green civil society in China. In: *State of the World 2006.* New York: W.W. Norton.

Lum, Thomas; Fischer, Hannah; Gomez-Granger, Julissa; and Leland, Anne (2009) *China's Foreign Aid Activities in Africa, Latin America and Southeast Asia.* Congressional Research Service. [online]. Available at: http://www.fas.org/sgp/crs/row/R40361.pdf (accessed January 7, 2012).

Ma, Bo (1996) *Blood Red Sunset: A Memoir of the Chinese Cultural Revolution.* Translated from the Chinese by Howard Goldblatt. London: Penguin.

Ma, Jun (2004) *China's Water Crisis.* Norwalk, CT: Eastbridge.

Ma, Tianjie (2008/2009) Environmental mass incidents in rural China: Examining large-scale unrest in Dongyang, Zhejiang. *China Environment Series,* 10: 33–56. Available at: http://www.wilsoncenter.org/sites/default/files/ces10.pdf (accessed January 7, 2012).

Ma, Wayne (2011) Sinopec's Galp deal deepens China-Brazil energy ties. *Dow Jones Newswires.* [online] November 10, 2011. Available at: http://online.wsj.com/article/BT-CO-20111110-724459.html (accessed January 7, 2012).

Ma, Xiaoying and Ortolano, Leonard (2000) *Environmental Regulation in China: Institutions, Enforcement, and Compliance.* Oxford: Rowman and Littlefield.

McDonough, William and Braungart, Michael (2002) *Cradle To Cradle: Remaking The Way We Make Things.* New York: North Point Press.

McElwee, Charles R. (2011) *Environmental Law in China: Managing Risk and Ensuring Compliance.* Oxford: Oxford University Press.

MacLeod, Calum (2011) China's organic farms rooted in food-safety concerns. *USA Today.* [online] January 23, 2011. Available at: http://www.usatoday.com/news/world/2011-01-24-chinafood24_ST_N.htm (accessed January 7, 2012).

Marcuse, Gary, director (2011) *Waking the Green Tiger* [film]. Vancouver: Face to Face Media.

Marks, Robert (2006) *Tigers, Rice, Silk, and Silt: Environment and Economy in Late Imperial South China*. Cambridge: Cambridge University Press.

Marston, Rebecca (2011) No rules for the rich: How China spends its new wealth. *BBC*. [online] May 11, 2011. Available at: http://www.bbc.co.uk/news/business-13284481 (accessed January 7, 2012).

Mastny, Lisa (ed.) (2010) *Renewable Energy and Energy Efficiency in China: Current Status and Prospects for 2020*. Washington, DC: Worldwatch Institute.

Mattheissen, Peter (1978) *The Snow Leopard*. New York: Viking.

Ministry of Commerce, People's Republic of China (2011) Statistics of China's Absorption of FDI from January to December 2010, http://english.mofcom.gov.cn/aarticle/statistic/foreigninvestment/201101/20110107381641.html (accessed January 7, 2012).

Minx, Jan C.; Baiocchi, Giovanni; Peters, Glen P.; Weber, Christopher L.; Guan, Dabo; and Hubacek, Klaus (2011) A "carbonizing dragon": China's fast growing CO_2 emissions revisited. *Environmental Science and Technology*, 45(21): 9144–53.

Mittelman, James H. (2000) *Globalization Syndrome*. Princeton, NJ: Princeton University Press.

Moore, Malcolm (2008) "China Plans Dams across Tibet." *The Telegraph*. [online] October 14. Available at: http://www.telegraph.co.uk/news/worldnews/asia/tibet/3193790/China-plans-dams-across-Tibet.html (accessed January 7, 2012).

Morton, Katherine (2005) *International Aid and China's Environment*. London: Taylor & Francis.

Murtha, Andrew (2008) *China's Water Warriors: Citizen Action and Policy Change*. Ithaca, NY: Cornell University Press.

Myers, Norman (1997) Environmental refugees. *Population and Environment*, 19(2): 167–82.

Needham, Joseph (multiple dates, 27 volumes) *Science and Civilization in China*. Cambridge: Cambridge University Press.

OECD (2007) *OECD Environmental Performance Review of China*. Paris: Organization for Economic Cooperation and Development. Available at: http://www.oecd.org/document/47/0,3343,en_2649_201185_37809647_1_1_1_1,00.html (accessed January 7, 2012).

Pan, Jiahua; Ma, Haibing; and Zhang, Ying (2011) *Green Economy and Green Jobs in China: Current Status and Potentials for 2020*. Washington, DC: Worldwatch Institute.

Paull, John (2007) China's organic revolution. *Journal of Organic Systems*, 2(1): 1–11.

Pierson, David (2011) Coal mining in China's Inner Mongolia fuels tensions. *The Los Angeles Times*. [online] June 2, 2011. Available at: http://articles.latimes.com/2011/jun/02/business/la-fi-china-coal-20110602 (accessed January 7, 2012).

Qu, Geping and Li, Jinchang (1994) *Population and the environment in China* [*Zhongguo renkou yu Huanjing*]. Boulder, CO: Lynne Rienner.

Rosenthal, Elizabeth (2011) Making headway in the movement to protect the world's sharks. *The New York Times*. [online] September 10, 2011. Available at: http://www.nytimes.com/2011/09/11/science/earth/11shark.html (accessed January 7, 2012).

Schaller, George (1993) *The Last Panda*. Chicago, IL: University of Chicago Press.

Schmalzer, Sigrid (2008) *The People's Peking Man: Popular Science and Human Identity in Twentieth-Century China*. Chicago, IL: University of Chicago Press.

Schuman, Michael (2011) China's mining pit. *TIME*. [online] June 19, 2011. Available at: http://www.time.com/time/printout/0,8816,2075236,00.html (accessed January 7, 2012).

Scott, James C. (1985) *Weapons of the Weak: Everyday Forms of Peasant Resistance*. New Haven, CT: Yale University Press.

Scott, James C. (1998) *Seeing Like a State: How Certain Schemes to Improve the Human Condition Have Failed*. New Haven, CT: Yale University Press.

Shalizi, Zmarak (2006) *Addressing China's Growing Water Shortages and Associated Social and Environmental Consequences*. Development Research Group, World Bank. [online]. Available at: http://siteresources.worldbank.org/INTEAPREGTOPENVIRONMENT/Resources/Addressing_China_Water_Scarcity_EN.pdf (accessed January 7, 2012).

Shapiro, Judith (2001) *Mao's War against Nature*. Cambridge: Cambridge University Press.

Sinkule, Barbara J. and Ortolano, Leonard (1995) *Implementing Environmental Policy in China*. Westport, CT: Praeger.

Stalley, Phillip (2010) *Foreign Firms, Investment, and Environmental Regulation in the People's Republic of China*. Stanford, CA: Stanford University Press.

State Council of the People's Republic of China (2011) White Paper on China's Policies and Actions for Addressing Climate Change. Full text available at: http://news.xinhuanet.com/english2010/china/2011-11/22/c_131262368.htm (accessed January 7, 2012).

State Environmental Protection Administration (2006) Green GDP accounting study report 2004 issued. Press release. [online] September 11, 2006.

Available at: http://english.gov.cn/2006-09/11/content_384596.htm (accessed January 7, 2012).

Stern, David (2003) Environmental Kuznets curve. *Internet Encyclopedia of Ecological Economics*. [online]. Available at: http://www.ecoeco.org/pdf/stern. pdf (accessed January 7, 2012).

Su, Xiaokang (1988) River Elegy. [film series] China.

Sui, Lee-wee (2011) China says will shut plant as thousands protest. *Reuters*. [online] August 14, 2011. Available at: http://in.reuters.com/ article/2011/08/14/idINIndia-58776820110814 (accessed January 7, 2012).

Sun, Chanjin; Chen, Liqiao; Chen, Lijun; and Bass, Steve (2008) *Global Forest Product Chains: Identifying Challenges and Opportunities for China through a Global Commodity Chain Sustainability Analysis*. International Institute for Sustainable Development. [online]. Available at: http://www.iisd.org/ publications/pub.aspx?id=1066 (accessed January 7, 2012).

Sun, Xiufang and Canby, Kerstin (2010) *China: Overview of Forest Governance, Markets and Trade*. Forest Trends. [online]. Available at: http://forest-trends.org/publication_details.php?publicationID=2878 (accessed January 7, 2012).

Taylor, Ian (2009) *China's New Role in Africa*. London: Lynne Rienner Publishers.

Theroux, Paul (1988) *Riding the Iron Rooster: By Train through China*. New York: Putnam's.

Thubron, Colin (1989) *Behind the Wall: A Journey through China*. New York: Atlantic Monthly Press.

Thubron, Colin (2007) *Shadow of the Silk Road*. London: Chatto & Windus.

United Nations Development Program (UNDP) (2011) *Sustainability and Equity: A Better Future for All* (Human Development Report 2011). New York: UNDP. Available at: http://hdr.undp.org/en/media/HDR_2011_ EN_Complete.pdf (accessed January 5, 2012).

United Nations Office of the High Commissioner for Human Rights (UNOHCHR) (2010) "From food security to the right to food" – UN expert highlights China's next steps. Press release [online] December 23, 2010. Available at: http://www.ohchr.org/en/NewsEvents/Pages/DisplayNews. aspx?NewsID=10612&LangID=E (accessed January 7, 2012).

U.S. Department of State (2010) *Report of the Visa Office*. Bureau of Consular Services. [online]. http://www.travel.state.gov/visa/statistics/statistics_5240. html. (accessed January 7, 2012).

U.S. Department of the Treasury (2011) *Major Foreign Holders of Treasury Securities*. [online]. Available at: http://www.treasury.gov/resource-center/ data-chart-center/tic/Documents/mfh.txt (accessed January 7, 2012).

U.S. Energy Information Administration (2010) *International Energy Outlook 2010*. [online] Available at: http://www.eia.gov/oiaf/archive/ieo10/index. html (accessed January 7, 2012).

Vermont Law School (2010) *U.S.-China Partnership for Environmental Law* [online]. Available at: http://www.vermontlaw.edu/x1463.xml (accessed January 7, 2012).

Voice of America (2011) Chinese VP pledges accelerated development in Tibet. [online] July 19, 2011. Available at: http://www.voanews.com/ tibetan-english/news/Chinese-VP-Pledges-Accelerated-Development-in-Tibet-125805533.html (accessed January 7, 2012).

Wallerstein, Immanuel (1979) *Capitalist World-Economy*. Cambridge: Cambridge University Press.

Wang, Alex (2006–2007) Role of law in environmental protection in China: Recent developments. *Vermont Journal of Environmental Law*, 8: 195–379. Available at: http://www.vjel.org/journal/VJEL10057.html (accessed January 7, 2012).

Wang, Alex (2011) Green courts serious step forward for cleaner China. *Global Times*. [online] September 28, 2011. Available at: http://www.globaltimes. cn/NEWS/tabid/99/ID/677512/Green-courts-serious-step-forward-for-cleaner-China.aspx (accessed January 7, 2012).

Wang, Xiaoyi (2007) *Undermining Grassland Management through Centralized Environmental Policies in Inner Mongolia*. World Resources Institute. [online]. Available at: http://pdf.wri.org/wp29_wxiaoyi.pdf (accessed January 7, 2012).

Wapner, Paul (1995) Politics beyond the state: Environmental activism and world civic politics. *World Politics*, 47(3): 311–40.

Watts, Jonathan (2010a) China's "cancer villages" reveal dark side of economic boom. *The Guardian*. [online] June 6, 2010. Available at: http://www. guardian.co.uk/environment/2010/jun/07/china-cancer-villages-industrial-pollution (accessed January 7, 2012).

Watts, Jonathan (2010b) *When a Billion Chinese Jump: How China Will Save Mankind – Or Destroy It*. New York: Simon & Schuster.

Watts, Jonathan (2011) China's love affair with the car shuns green vehicles. *The Guardian*. [online] August 24, 2011. Available at: http://www.guardian.co. uk/environment/2011/aug/24/china-cars-green-vehicles (accessed January 7, 2012).

Wedeman, Andrew (2009) Enemies of the state: Mass incidents and subversion in China. In: American Political Science Association, *Annual Meeting*. Toronto, September 2009. Available at: http://papers.ssrn.com/sol3/papers. cfm?abstract_id=1451828 (accessed January 7, 2012).

Weller, Robert P. (2006) *Discovering Nature: Globalization and Environmental Culture in China and Taiwan.* Cambridge: Cambridge University Press.

White Jr., Lynn T. (1967) The historical roots of our ecological crisis. *Science,* 155(3767): 1203–7.

Wines, Michael (2011) Bystanders' neglect of injured toddler sets off soul-searching on web sites in China. *New York Times.* [online] October 18, 2011. Available at: http://www.nytimes.com/2011/10/19/world/asia/toddlers-accident-sets-off-soul-searching-in-china.html?pagewanted=all (accessed January 7, 2012).

Wines, Michael and Jonathan Ansfield (2010) Trampled in a land rush, Chinese resist. *New York Times.* [online] May 26, 2010. Available at: http://www.nytimes.com/2010/05/27/world/asia/27china.html (accessed January 7, 2012).

Wittfogel, Karl (1957) *Oriental Despotism: A Comparative Study of Total Power.* New Haven, CT: Yale University Press.

Woetzel, Jonathan; Mendonca, Lenny; Devan, Janamitra; Negri, Stefano; Hu, Yamgei; Jordan, Luke; Li, Xiujun; Maasry, Alexander; Tsen, Geoff; and Yu, Flora (2009) *Preparing for China's Urban Billion.* McKinsey Global Institute. [online]. Available at: http://www.mckinsey.com/Insights/MGI/Research/Urbanization/Preparing_for_urban_billion_in_China (accessed January 7, 2012).

World Bank (2011) China | Data. [online]. Available at: http://data.worldbank.org/country/china (accessed January 7, 2012).

World Commission on Environment and Development (WCED) (1987) *Our Common Future.* Oxford: Oxford University Press.

World Nuclear Association (2011) *Nuclear Power in China.* [online]. Available at: http://www.world-nuclear.org/info/inf63.html (accessed January 7, 2012).

World Resources Institute (1999) *China's Health and Environment: Air Pollution and Health Effects.* [online]. Available at: http://www.wri.org/publication/content/8416 (accessed January 7, 2012).

World Trade Organization (WTO) (2011) *China Trade Profile.* [online]. Available at: http://stat.wto.org/CountryProfile/WSDBCountryPFView.aspx?Language=E&Country=CN (accessed January 7, 2012).

Wu, Fengshi (2002) New partners or old brothers? GONGOs in transnational environmental advocacy in China. *China Environment Series,* 5: 47–53.

Wu, Wencong (2011) E-waste still fuels pollution, says NGO. *China Daily.* [online] May 9, 2011. Available at: http://www.chinadaily.com.cn/cndy/2011-05/09/content_12467241.htm (accessed January 7, 2012).

Xie, Jian (2009) *Addressing China's Water Scarcity: Recommendations for Selected Water Resource Management Issues.* World Bank. [online]. Available at: http://

www-wds.worldbank.org/external/default/WDSContentServer/WDSP/ IB/2009/01/14/000333037_20090114011126/Rendered/PDF/471110P UB0CHA0101OFFICIAL0USE0ONLY1.pdf (accessed January 7, 2012).

Xie, Xiaoping (2011) Apple breaks its silence. *China Dialogue* [online] October 3, 2011. Available at: http://www.chinadialogue.net/article/show/single/en/4561 (accessed January 7, 2012).

Yang, Ruby, director (2010) *Warriors of Qiugang* [film]. Beijing: Thomas Lennon Films & Chang Ai Media Project.

Yeh, Emily (2009) Greening western China: A critical view. *Geoforum*, 40(5): 884–94.

Zheng, Yisheng and Qian, Yihong (1998) *Grave Concerns – Problems of Sustainable Development in China* [*Shendu Youhuan: Dangdai Zhongguo de Kechixu Fazahan Wenti*]. Beijing: Jinri Zhongguo Chubanshe.

Zhou, Yinghua (2002) Report on China's development and investment in land and water. Proceedings of the Regional Consultation. Bangkok, Thailand, October 3–5, 2001. Food and Agriculture Organization of the United Nations Regional Office for Asia and Pacific: Bangkok. Available at: http://www.fao.org/docrep/005/ac623e/ac623e0d.htm (accessed January 7, 2012).

Index